TRENDS AND TRIPWIRES 3

DEBUNKING THE RANDOM WALK

Other books by this author:

TRENDS AND TRIPWIRES

Wright Books (An Imprint of John Wiley & Sons)

First Published 2001

.

TRENDS AND TRIPWIRES 2 – RANDOM? NOT RANDOM

First Published 2005

www.trendsandtripwires.com

Trends and Tripwires 3 is dedicated to Louise, Kimberley, Adam and Nikki.

Thank you to www.spacejock.com for their kind permission to use screen shots. I am a licensed user of the remarkable FCharts Pro charting software.

Thank you to www.barchart.com for their kind permission to use screen shots from their web site and also the excellent barchart app.

First Printing 2016

ISBN 978-1-329-85544-1

Trends and Tripwires

www.trendsandtripwires.com

Perth Western Australia

VERY IMPORTANT!

It is essential that readers obtain the TT3 overlay tool in order to fully appreciate and understand the method described here. The tool can be ordered inexpensively from the web site at   www.trendsandtripwires.com

QUICK START GUIDE

I know when something new arrives in the mail we just want to get right into it and not worry about having to read the manual first. This is why I have prepared this quick start guide for you. The main section of Trends and Tripwires 3 will present a more thorough explanation of the TT3 overlay but for now the following information should get readers started.

It is important to note that these books and overlay tools are intended for educational purposes. The Trends and Tripwires books present readers with an opportunity to see what they are up against when choosing to trade in financial markets, it is similar to playing chess against a computer, so please beware!

The TT3 is the latest in a series of overlay tools that began with the original Trends and Tripwires book way back in 2001. The TT3 has a series of equally spaced lines with five coloured lines nearest to the centre. The five coloured lines can be used (but not essentially) to enclose a breakout trend in any liquid share chart and the additional lines are there to assist in accurately placing the overlay. The nine lines represent a part segment from a geometric grid that is proposed to exist on major league trader's charts. The theory is that by reproducing their grid as accurately as possible we can become acutely aware of their activity and as the big money totally dominates financial markets the information gleaned from the TT3 can be very revealing.

Image A has been enclosed with grid lines from the TT3 overlay. The reader should start by placing the TT3 in the same position on the chart. Notice that the central (coloured) lines enclose a breakout section and the upper and lower outer lines have been used to carefully locate the TT3. The image is not perfect but it is pretty accurate. This is because the TT3 overlay is attempting to emulate an invisible grid I believe to be located on major league trading computers somewhere else in the world. It is our job to recreate this grid and hopefully respond appropriately to its signals.

Image A is displayed with the apex of the TT3 pointing upwards, it is interesting to note that it is sometimes easier for beginners to place the TT3 with the apex pointing down. The overlay tool can be used on literally thousands of financial charts from all over the world.

Some charts will display the grid very obviously and these are the examples to pursue first. If the grid is not obvious on the chart being tracked then it is probably wiser to move to a better image. Always look for a chart with fully formed price bars and not with dashes representing very low volume as these are too difficult to track. Intraday, daily weekly and monthly charts can all be enclosed with the overlay, its ratios are visible everywhere as they have already been imposed on price bar data probably by an external computer.

Image A

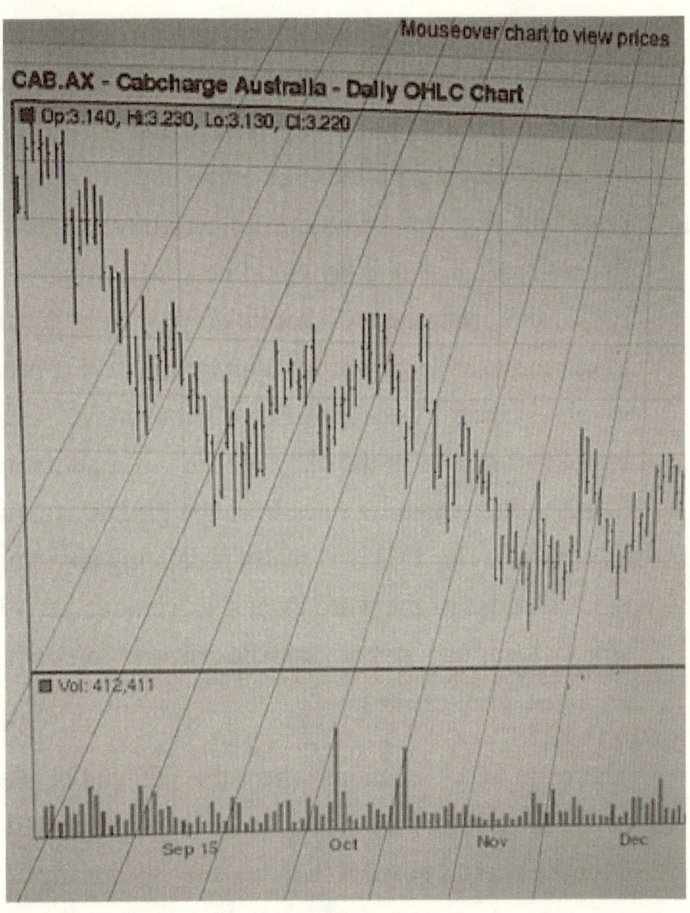

Unfortunately it is not known exactly what timescale the remote chart or grid is using. Is it 100 days or fifty weeks or 36 months? Fortunately because the remote computer has already imposed its activities on this and most other world charts for many years, we can use its past activity to project future grid lines and the time scale is not super critical.

Notice particularly where the navigation points or corners in the chart are and also critically, the angles created by runs of price bars as in Image A. These indicate unseen grid lines that either support or resist price bars that very often line up perfectly and dutifully like soldiers. The overlay could be used by tracking backwards from the most recent activity or by locating a past move and projecting it forwards. Each approach involves carefully enclosing an obvious move within two TT3 lines, as in the diagrams and then attempting to place the remaining lines from the grid as accurately as possible. The TT3 isn't really predicting anything in the true sense of the word even if it seems to be, it is simply locating a remote trader's grid and forecasting its future implications.

There are many locations where the TT3 can be placed as the fixed ratios are evident and can be measured all over the chart. I suspect that this enables trading computers to operate in a controlled environment, measuring ratios in the data and placing buy and sells at specific trigger points. The TT3 can be used on intraday, daily, weekly and monthly charts. As the overlay is measuring pre imposed ratios or distances between trends, the chart scaling is not a huge issue, but still something to be considered. For instance in Forex trading around the time of an important announcement, a move could be in the order of hundreds of pips and this will certainly compress and distort a chart massively. In most normal situations however the chart can be analysed without a problem when there is a moderate degree of distortion.

An experienced analyst can surely already understand the implications of what I am proposing here. Predictable ratios are very often useful indicators of future activity. It is wholly understandable if this seems to be an improbable suggestion, but the evidence is undeniable and indeed discoverable in almost any world financial chart, including shares, currencies, commodities etc. Contrary to almost universal professional opinion, financial markets are clearly not at all random.

Image B

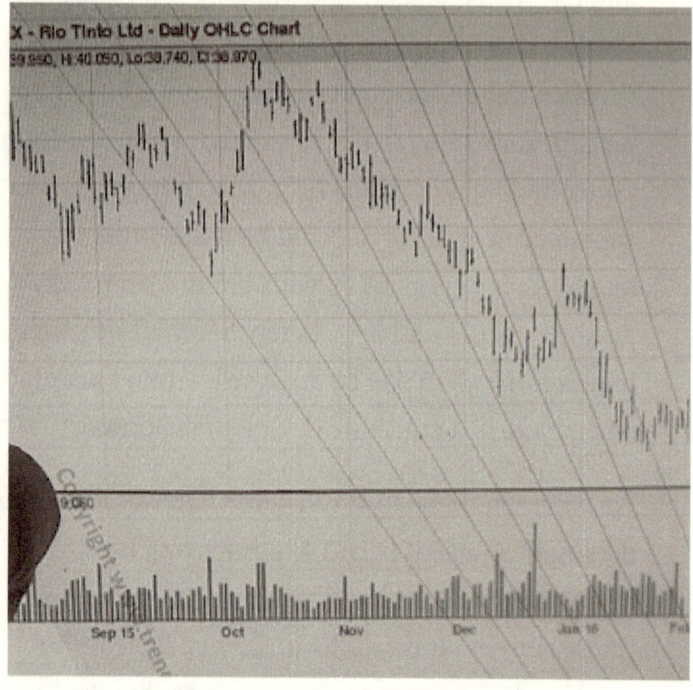

Image B features a six month chart of RIO (for no particular reason) using the TT3 apex at the bottom and therefore identifying likely tripwires. When these tripwires are broken there are opportunities to chart several short term rallies. The TT3 overlay presents the reader with a far more orderly representation of any chart. Without the TT3 analysis tool the chart seems random and neurotic, but the activity is not at all as random as it appears to be at first glance.

Some of the enclosed examples in the quick start section are displayed on 3-6 month daily charts and this seems to be one good place to start. It is also a good idea to begin by using the TT3 with the apex at the bottom in a kind of down trending approach. It is sometimes easier to place the TT3 in this way because the downward moves tend to persist. Image C offers an excellent example of this approach and once the user has placed around two or three TT3 lines, a fairly accurate prediction emerges of likely future breakouts.

Image C shows a fairly common representation of the TT3 when used for planning breakouts. It has been located by enclosing the extremities of the first downtrend on the leftmost side of the chart within two TT3 lines. Potential breakouts are then located at fairly predictable slices of time, perhaps revealing a trading computer's likely trigger points.

The SECOND TT3 line from the left is VERY important and it is necessary to take careful note of the slope of this line and how it has been located. This second line is often the key to locating the rest of the grid, as the other lines from the TT3 are relative to this line in terms of angles and slices of time. Existing trend angles give the analyst an idea of the volatility of this chart and even at what angle future activity might eventuate. The same TT3 lines also warn the analyst where the next trigger points are most likely to be.

Image C

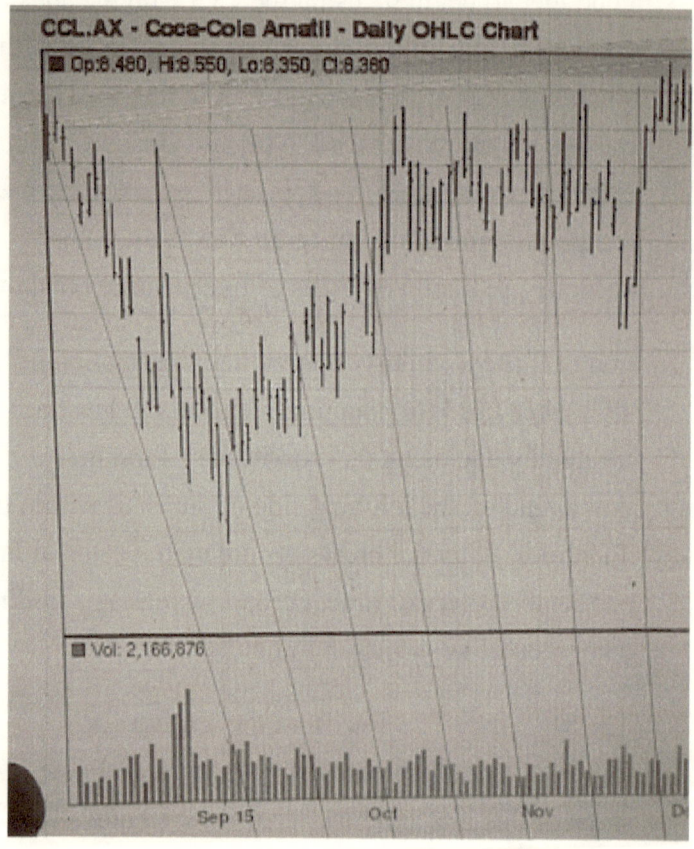

Image D

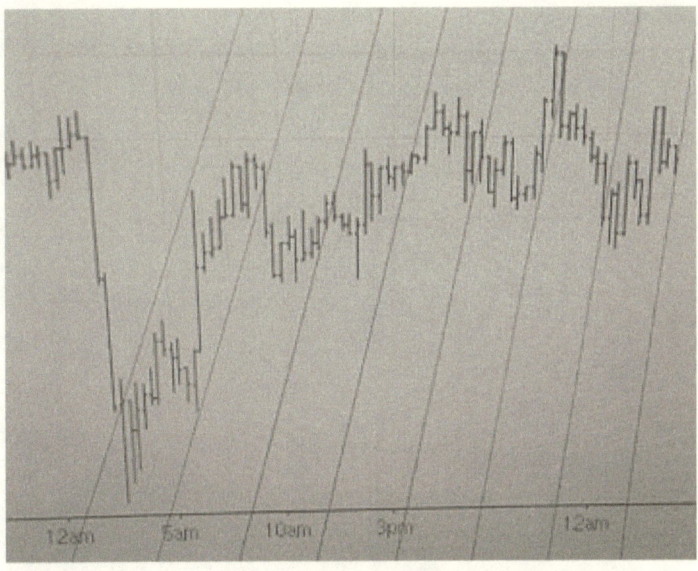

The images (D & E) are intraday FX charts and display
a 20 minute tick chart of AUDJPY. The TT3 has been
particularly useful in these examples and has been used
to "predict" future trend triggers and angles quite
successfully. Again the TT3 encloses significant
moves and as the new price bars arrive the overlay is
tweaked slightly until the forthcoming grid lines offer
a useful projection of future activity.

IMAGE E

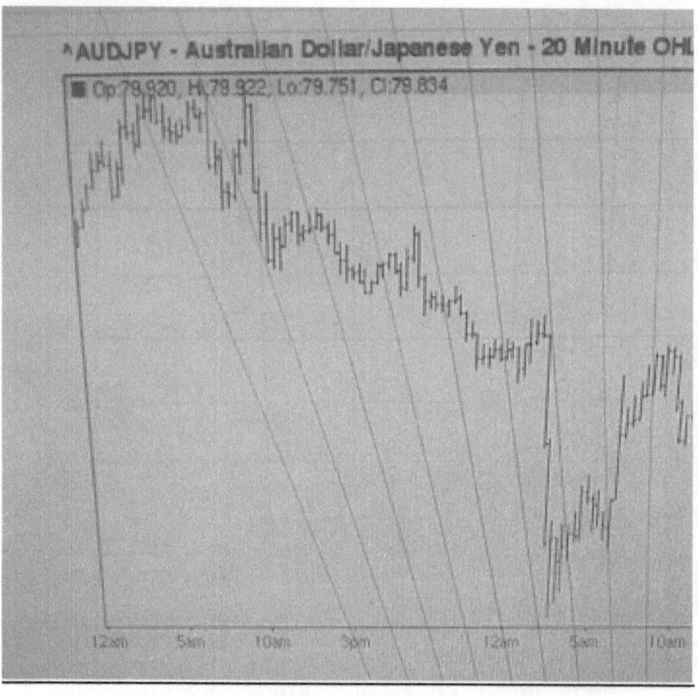

Another way to start with the TT3 is to use a chart with obvious corners or turning points in the data. I refer to these as navigation points because they offer evidence of the location of the current grid we are looking for. I have chosen a 1 minute chart for this example and displayed around 5-6 hours of price bars. It is very interesting to note how much this chart resembles a typical daily or weekly chart as the ratios we are measuring are still clearly evident. I have found that an excellent way to practice the Trends and Tripwires method is to download "Metatrader 5" or "Myfxbook" or similar free for your phone or tablet (Google Play). This will provide a demo account where the user can perfect skills without fear of financial loss. These app charts work beautifully with the TT3 too as a bonus.

For another quick start approach the user could first choose a recent and obvious peak (pivot) and the angle after the next low as in images (F&G).

See-saw this peak with the top or leftmost TT3 line. Now rotate and align the critical SECOND TT3 line under the following valley low, and align it with the angle created by the next few price bar lows. Now the third TT3 line and maybe the fourth and fifth will "predict" the next possible trigger point and also its trend angle! It will probably be necessary to tweak the TT3 slightly if and when the trigger occurs (make it a little wider). Don't expect 100% accuracy with your analysis lines, they will not be perfect but they will be pretty close. The predicted trend line is both a support line and stop loss line simultaneously. If it has been placed correctly, any break of the line may cause a significant reaction and not necessarily pleasant! These projected TT3 lines must be treated with great respect, they have the potential to make or break your day.

IMAGE (F)

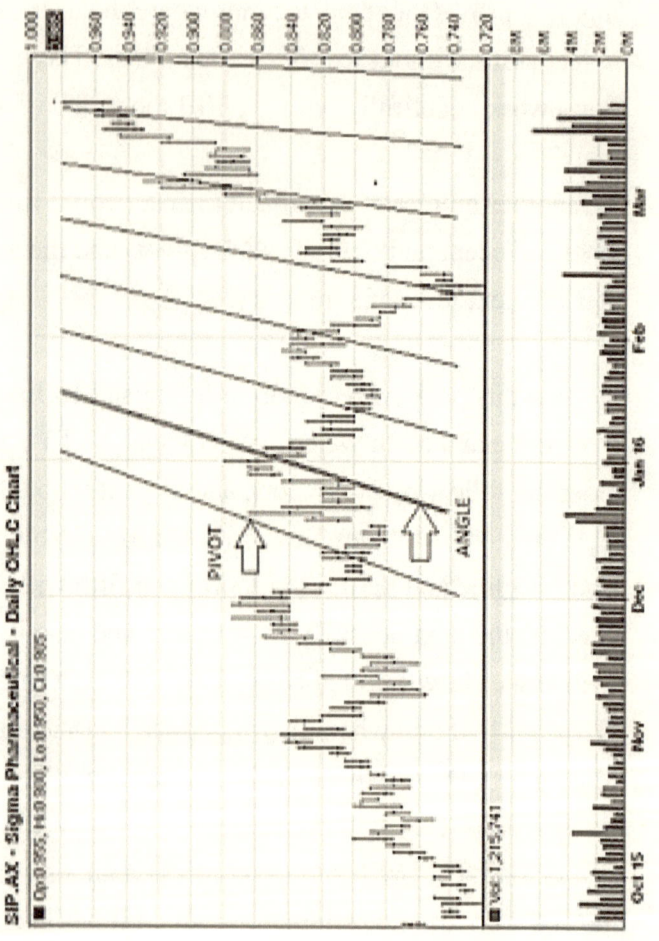

IMAGE (G)

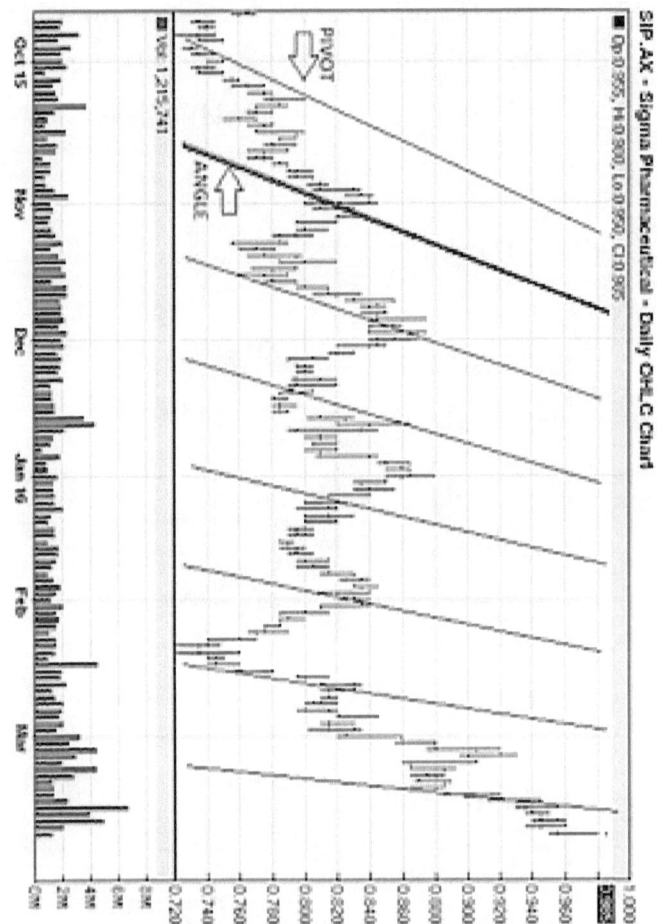

The following two images are 30 day charts of CSL showing that the TT3 lines can be aligned in more than one way. The user can take a reference from a recent slope as in the upper example, or a recent move can be enclosed in two TT3 lines and projected forward.

CSL 30 DAY CHARTS

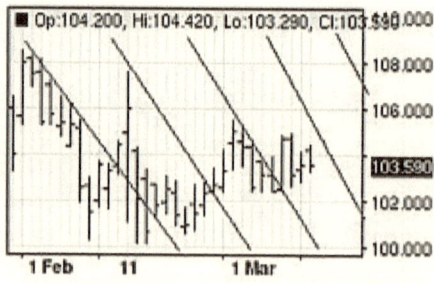

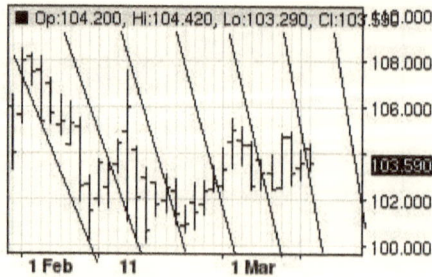

IMAGE (H) 15 MINUTE INTRADAY CHART

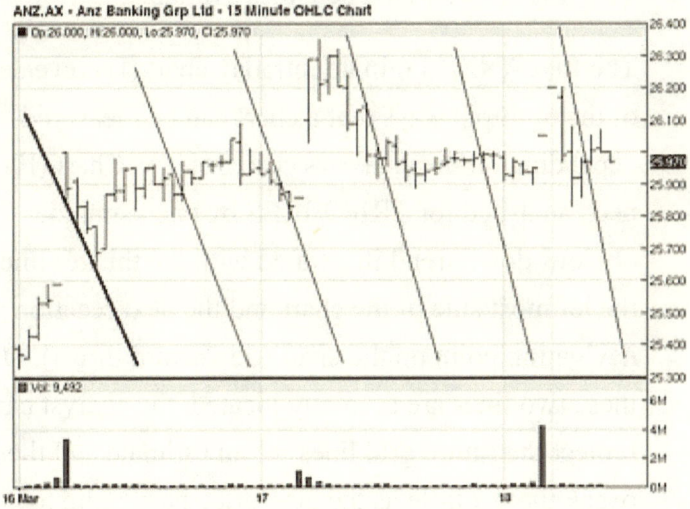

ANZ.AX - Anz Banking Grp Ltd - 15 Minute OHLC Chart

This study will show readers how to place TT3 lines in multiple ways on the same intraday chart. Some people have asked me why the overlay is not currently provided in software and some of the reasons are as you will see here, the chart would become very complex very quickly, with multiple trends and tripwires obscuring the required information. The TT3 will be available in existing technical analysis software soon however.

The TT3 overlay is a separate tool that works in a similar way to Gann and Fibonacci lines but with the advantage of greater accuracy, it measures geometric retracement levels and the ratios between trends. It is also necessary to measure the ratios in several directions and then continuously tweak (or widen) the TT3 lines as new data becomes available.

The first ANZ 15 minute intraday chart (H) reveals one of the multiple ways that a chart can be measured depending on the analyst's current view. Chart (H) has been analysed for TRIPWIRES by enclosing the obvious down trend illustrated with the thicker line on the leftmost side of the chart and the next reaction or navigation point on the chart (downward thrust). Once these two lines are correctly located, the analyst can project the future grid lines for an estimate and then tweak them a little as the new price bars begin to appear. Once the first three lines from the left are in place, the analyst has a good impression where the forthcoming downward reaction points are very likely to be. These future reaction points are demonstrated with the three lines on the rightmost side of the chart. Two out of these three lines produced a significant reaction and the TT3 warned us in advance.

IMAGE (I) 15 MINUTE INTRADAY CHART

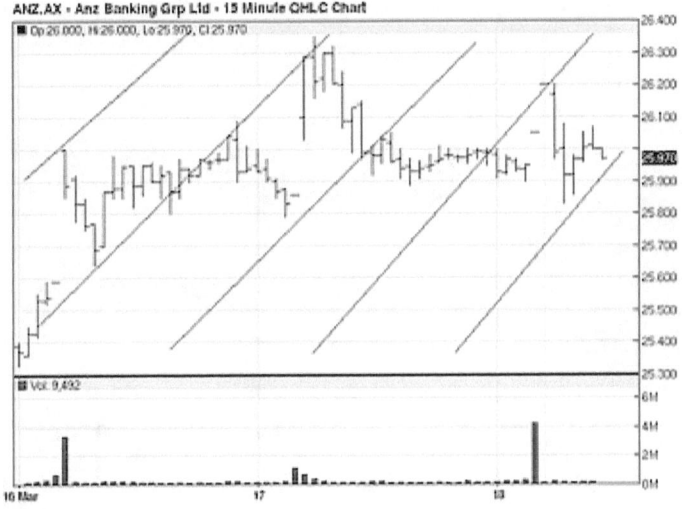

ANZ.AX - Anz Banking Grp Ltd - 15 Minute OHLC Chart

IMAGE (I) offers a different perspective on the same intraday chart and illustrates likely support levels after enclosing the early trend activity in the first two leftmost lines. Notice how the second line has been adjusted to roughly touch the high near the centre of the chart. Future likely support levels or TRENDS can then be projected from these two early lines. As price bars begin to appear the TT3 can be adjusted to confirm the grid's correct location.

IMAGE (J) 15 MINUTE INTRADAY CHART

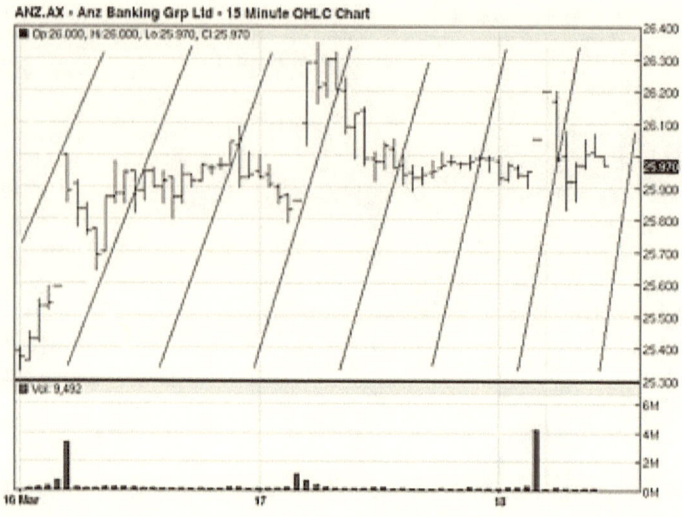

ANZ.AX - Anz Banking Grp Ltd - 15 Minute OHLC Chart

Image (J) is another representation of the same intraday chart and this time the ratios have been measured at a more extreme angle. These projected TRENDS derived from trigger points show evidence that our ratios can be measured in multiple ways. Example (J) offers some opportunities for those with an appetite for risk as the very short term trends are triggered at regular and predictable intervals.

Hopefully it is clearer now how ratios can be measured with the TT3 overlay. From intraday through to monthly and even yearly charts the ratios are just as evident and measurable offering a surprising degree of predictability to any analyst.

TRENDS AND TRIPWIRES 3

Trends and Tripwires 3 is not too surprisingly the third book in the series and this latest edition is primarily intended for use as a user manual for the newest TT3 overlay tool. This new A4 sized laminated overlay tool is the result of 16 years of intense research and whilst it might not look particularly exciting, its application to almost any liquid financial chart offers an extraordinary insight into the underlying geometry that drives past and even dare I say future price activity.

A casual observer might quite reasonably ask how this could be so. How can geometry possibly be of any value in a supposedly RANDOM bar chart? Furthermore when there are so many financial instruments of all denominations originating from all corners of the globe, how can anyone claim to have developed a tool that can be applied to almost any of these charts?

In order to answer such questions it is necessary to think outside the box for a moment. What is it that connects all of these technical analysis charts together? Is there some common denominator that may be relevant to all liquid financial charts? Are technical charts operating in some kind of controlled environment? The answer to these fully justified questions is likely to be found in a modern world controlled by computers and more particularly in this case with major league trading software. I say likely because I have never actually witnessed first- hand such software in action and can only assume that the non-random activity of a typical chart has been aggressively shaped by some computer somewhere. The reader could be forgiven for imagining that we may be living within the constraints of a programmed economy, a world where the price of oil or gold or whatever can be adjusted at the click of a mouse.

We are not talking about conspiracy theories here, I am not in any way proposing that a group of individuals have colluded to maintain an advantage for the few at the expense of the many. I am simply proposing that a geometrical framework does indeed exist for some perhaps inexplicable reason and that all analysts need to be aware of it (a level playing field). Just follow the information herein and readers will undoubtedly reach their own conclusions.

I am sure that once the reader has applied the TT3 overlay tool to dozens of charts and all by applying the exact methods described herein, then readers will gradually become convinced that this is indeed the case and that geometry can certainly be used to track financial chart activity, often with astonishing accuracy (even if it does fly in the face of trader logic). Sometimes traders are guilty of thinking way too smart and attempt to apply complex mathematical theories to issues with truly simple solutions.

This book is packed full of images of historical charts complete with lines traced by using the overlay as a template. The user should simply place the overlay on the computer screen, tablet or printed chart and either photograph the chart with their favourite smartphone (quick and convenient/ upload to share etc.), or using the computer mouse and technical analysis software, "trend lines" can be traced under the overlay tool to correspond with its printed lines. The latter method offers the advantage of watching the reactions to these and FUTURE lines as the chart progresses and new bars are added each day. It is remarkable to watch price bars bouncing on the projected future "trend lines," which began their life by hanging in white space on the right hand side of our computer monitor. This activity calls into question what trend lines actually are in this context. Are they one of a statistician's favourite mathematical tools? Or are they simply grid lines that have been incorporated into a computer algorithm? A programmed grid where price bars bounce up and down within the spaces between the boundary (trend) lines like a pin ball bouncing on the bumpers.

The more charts I analysed over the last sixteen years, the more I came to realize that the scale of the chart is a lot less of an issue than might be imagined. This is because the overlay is measuring RATIOS that have already been imposed on the chart most likely by computer software. That is to say that each price bar and each trend is mathematically related to other price bars and trends on the same chart, we are simply predicting where future grid lines will occur by taking a reference from the earlier lines.

Imagine first (as in Image 1) a series of vertical grid lines on the computer screen (with no price bars displayed). Now further imagine just for the sake of argument that the distance between any two grid lines on the screen is fixed at say 2cm. It is therefore not too difficult to work out/measure where the next grid line will occur, clearly 2cm away and the next line will be 4cm, 6cm, 8cm away etc. In reality the distance is not fixed in this way it varies considerably according to the size and placement of the grid. It is actually dictated by simple ratios as we shall soon see and it is the overlay's job to measure these ratios for us. If the first gap is say 3cm wide then the following gaps will be 6 cm, 9 cm, and 12 cm. Critically the distance between the following lines in the series depends on the distance between the first two lines.

One of the advantages of the overlay is that it can measure the ratios between trends or groups of price bars at any location on the screen, they don't have to be a series of vertical grid lines as in the previous example. They can also be a series of grid lines at 45 degrees to the horizontal or 60 degrees or whatever and we can still easily and quickly measure the regular distance between them. Images 1 and two will hopefully clarify this idea. I suspect that some high end software somewhere overlays fixed 360 degree wheels on most if not all financial charts at regular intervals. This creates recurring parallels and angles (the original Trends and Tripwires book from 2001 describes this) and also fixed recurring ratios on the price bars.

This book is not intended as a typical trading manual, it is an educational user guide for the TT3 overlay. Its intention is to show any aspiring trader what they are up against.

IMAGE 1

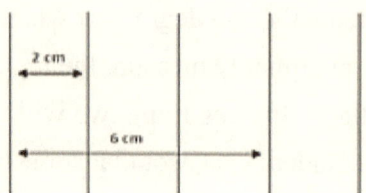

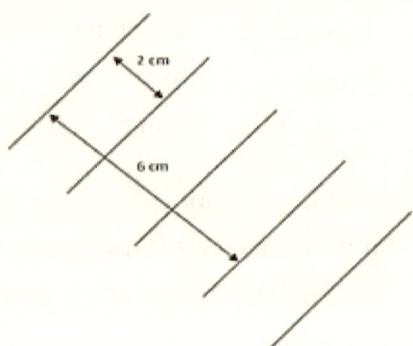

The scaling of the chart is an issue but much less of an issue than it might appear to be and this can be easily proven by purposely distorting the vertical or horizontal axis considerably by stretching the chart out.

IMAGE 2

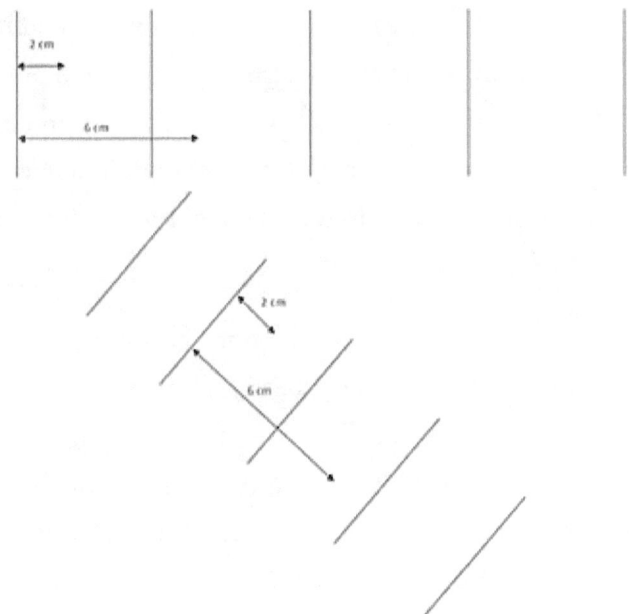

Clearly the distances have changed considerably from the previous example, but the RATIOS from gap to gap are the same (1:1, 2:1, 3:1, 4:1 etc.).Therefore stretching the chart horizontally or vertically doesn't really make much difference to the ratios we are measuring. Of course if the chart is massively distorted it will make it difficult to read and analyse, but the point I am making is that the overlay tool is measuring the distance between the first two grid lines and using a multiple of this to project the following lines and gaps. There is a very logical reason for this and it is because most financial charts appear to have been herded and shaped by one or more fixed geometric grids probably on a major league trader's screen and the overlay is used to recreate a portion of this highly influential grid.

Now if we imagine that the price bars are actually herded into position by these grid lines, the analysis method begins to make sense. By measuring the ratios between the grid lines we are also including the price bars in the analysis because the price bars align with the grid lines. In fact I could even go so far as to say that it is my belief that the trend lines that we are so fond of in technical analysis actually ARE these grid lines. Why would a series of price bars line up so dutifully like soldiers on a parade ground, unless they were controlled in some way? Perhaps not controlled with the intent to manipulate or deceive, but controlled even inadvertently by a software grid that encloses and herds price bars, almost magnetically attracting them to it. Fortunately the grid leaves significant evidence of its existence and historical charts can be carefully analysed for tell-tale signs. It will be revealed later in this guide that the longest term charts (5-10 years and more) can be especially useful because they tend to predict the most significant, long lasting and hopefully therefore reliable trends. As we progress we will also discuss TRIPWIRES and how to plot their likely locations. Strangely it is easier to track these down trends because they have a tendency to persevere, conveniently leaving significant navigation points on the chart that are very useful for tracking. From my own research I know that sometimes it is tempting to ignore a forthcoming tripwire, especially when there is a positive view about the chart's potential. However both TRENDS and TRIPWIRES need to be treated with great respect as they have the potential to make or break your day.

In the next two images 3 and 4 the same chart takes on an entirely different appearance when some TT3 overlay lines have been traced. It now appears to be a lot more predictable and seems to have been shaped/influenced by some kind of grid and the TT3 overlay tool represents our reproduction of at least a part of this grid that we can use for our own purposes.

IMAGE 3

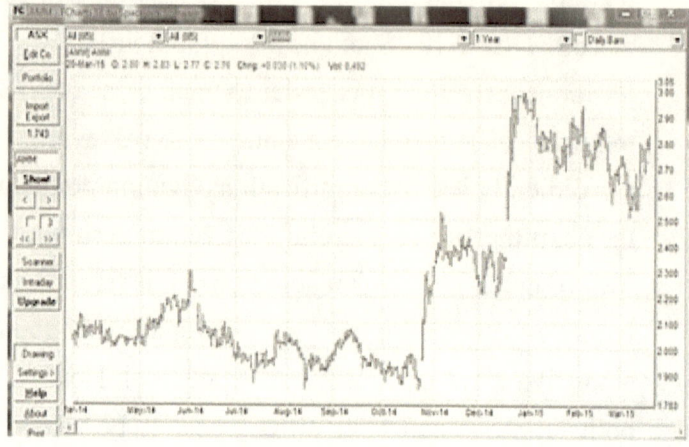

IMAGE 4

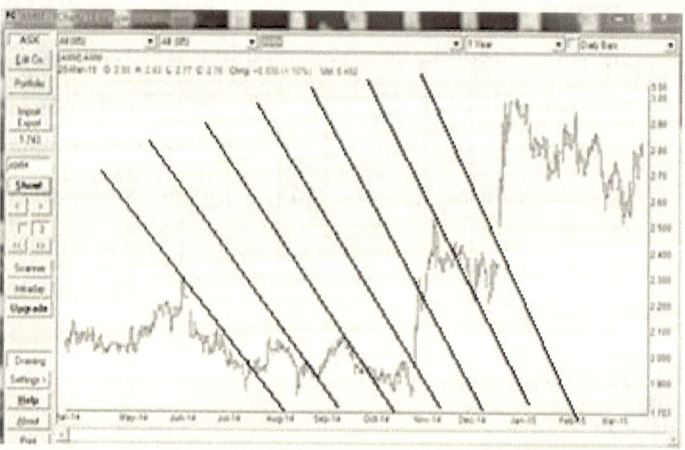

Strictly speaking, a grid should be a regular crisscross pattern of rising and falling lines but this can quickly begin to look too complicated on a financial chart and generally we are either primarily interested in the rising trend lines (TRENDS) which can also be used as stop loss lines when correctly placed and separately, the falling trend lines (TRIPWIRES) which are likely to disturb or brutally end our rising trend. Once the reader is aware of these recurring ratios the eye can be trained to recognise them when the overlay is not to hand. This is useful of course but the overlay delivers a degree of accuracy (not perfect) that is not available to the naked eye and should always be applied for confirmation. There are a great many charts in this book that have been enclosed with the overlay's grid lines and as the reader progresses the analysis method should become second nature. Try placing the TT3 overlay on many of these charts to measure for yourself and no doubt you will find that the tool becomes indispensable.

IMAGE 5

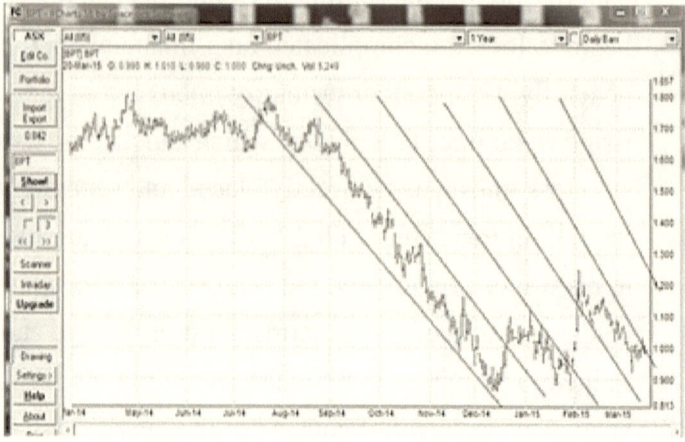

Image 5 has been enclosed within the guide lines as normal and the reader is encouraged to place the overlay on the chart in the same way as the example lines. It should align pretty well with the printed image. (There is more than one way to place the grid and your choice of location will depend on your perspective, time frame and how your knowledge of the technique develops).

IMAGE 6

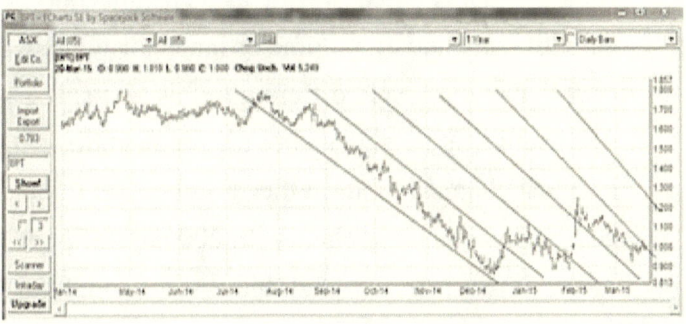

This time in image 6 the previous image (5) has been squashed quite significantly to the point where the trends have changed angles, but if the reader again places the overlay on the chart it is clear that the ratios have barely changed at all. Therefore it is not likely to pose a huge problem when using charts with a different scaling because even though the chart looks completely different, the ratios between the trends haven't changed (because the spacings on the grid don't change).

In fact it is sometimes quite revealing to stretch a chart, particularly vertically because a boring low volatility example can be easier to track when the price activity is exaggerated. The highs and valley lows appear to be more volatile which makes the chart easier to track. Usually this will not make much difference to the ratios being measured. The optimum though when possible, is to display a chart that is around 2:1, a rectangle that is twice as wide as its height (not including any add on volume or indicator windows). A chart that is massively different to this will still give very useful trigger signals but the trend angles will have just changed a bit. In the earlier books I recommended a daily chart with 200 days of price bars for maximum accuracy and this is still valid, but I have since found that because consecutive trend angles are relative by 2.5 degrees, the TT3 does a pretty good job of locating the next most likely trigger point and subsequent trend angle (so it is not necessary to stress too much about the time scale). This is provided of course that the user has carefully located around three earlier navigation points and is confident of the grid's location. The TT3 is equally at home with intraday, daily, weekly and monthly charts, probably because a similar grid is used by major league traders to enclose the price bars on these charts and it is our job to try and replicate it.

It is more revealing to make the chart smaller than to try to view it on the latest wide screen monitor, as the relationships between the trends are more obvious on smaller charts (particularly tiny charts).

Any LIQUID intraday chart with fully formed price bars is very revealing as the user can place the overlay over the chart and then watch the future price bars magically align with its grid lines, a kind of real time lesson that is a sure fire confidence builder. Once the user has witnessed this almost real time activity on an intraday chart, it is easier to imagine a similar phenomenon developing on daily, weekly and monthly charts as the method is very much the same but in slow motion. It is often easiest at first to align the TT3 with the tripwires (or down trending lines) as they tend to persist and seem to be more obviously cooperating with the overlay. The navigation points are also more obvious.

PLACING THE TT3 OVERLAY

There is a degree of skill involved in placing the overlay, particularly if you are new to the process, but like most pursuits a little practice goes a long way. It is a good idea to place the overlay on every chart you are currently tracking and also those from the past if you still have them. It is easiest to use the TT3 on a tablet computer or a reasonable sized smart phone. A laptop also works just fine but the image is sometimes a bit too big for the overlay. I would therefore suggest REDUCING the size of the chart possibly by about a half or more. I know most people prefer to display the largest chart possible, but as you will hopefully see, a lot of information can be lost in this way. Relationships between trends are much easier to measure when the chart is smaller and I know that this might sound counter intuitive, but with this method it is indeed the case. In fact when analysing long term charts of five or ten years duration, it can be extremely revealing to place the overlay on a TINY chart, but more on this later.

Initial study of the chart will reveal various "navigation points" in the data. These may be a particularly spikey price bar that stands out from the crowd or perhaps an obvious corner in the price activity where price bars suddenly take a new direction. Usually a small run of price bars will create an obvious angle on screen as if they have been herded into position. They have most probably been herded by a grid line, perhaps on a major trader's chart somewhere. It is our job to attempt to recreate this grid in an attempt to understand how the major players are analysing this chart. By recognising these angles and sudden changes of direction, it is possible to gain an insight into where the remote grid is located and the TT3 overlay tool was designed for this. This kind of clue helps the user to carefully place the overlay as ACCURATELY as possible. Even with the greatest care though it is still possible to misjudge a trend or a tripwire by a period or two, but the more navigation points that correctly and clearly align on the chart, the more likely that the grid has been placed correctly. As we progress through this guide and increase our detail and accuracy, readers will be convinced that most if not all world financial charts are dominated by a grid with very similar spacing to our overlay tool. Where a trend is wide it is because the grid spacing is wider (so just slide the TT3 up a little until it fits) and similarly when a trend is narrow, then the remote grid spacings are also narrow.

SIGNIFICANT GRID ANGLE PROJECTIONS

(ON THE SAME 30 DAY APPLE INC. CHART)

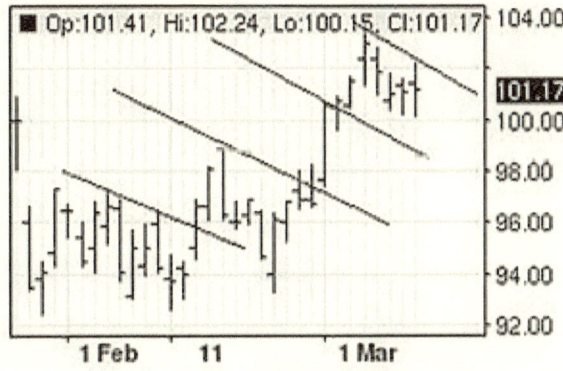

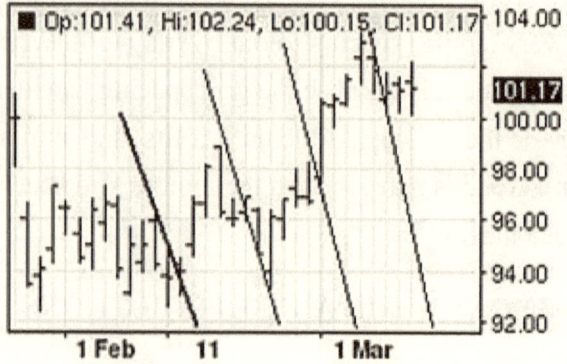

In Image 7 (a and b) there are two very obvious highs, a few other highs and four or five obvious lows. There are also several significant corners, valley lows and angles and these are all useful in helping us to place the overlay and I usually refer to these as "navigation points."

IMAGE 7a - WITHOUT TT3 LINES.

IMAGE 7b - WITH TT3 LINES

Once a set of TT3 lines are traced on the chart the situation becomes a little clearer and the image no longer seems to be so random. Price bars are aggressively shaped and herded by the grid lines and activity appears to be subject to computer control.

Sometimes the wider end of the overlay is easier to use at first, because we are mainly looking for major turning points and don't need so much detail at this stage. It is quite possible to progress to a more detailed analysis by zooming in to price bar activity using the narrower end of the TT3 (the apex). At this stage though it is most important to take careful measurements of newly forming trend angles at major turning points, as these sudden short term advances or declines are very useful navigation points.

Remember that what we are trying to do is recreate part of a grid as displayed on some major league player's computer somewhere and the overlay tool when correctly placed will do just that. The advantage of this is that the reader will now be aware of the huge impact these traders have on the activity of any chart (which actually amounts to total domination). It will also allow you to attempt to mimic what they do but on a much smaller scale of course. There is no way to swim against their tide, they have unlimited ammunition and all we can hope to do is go with the flow.

Firstly it is necessary to analyse the angles created by earlier price bars (this angle and subsequent angles as we progress down the trend, will identify a portion of a grid probably from a significant trader's chart somewhere), so if we start with the first steep downtrend which began in early November 2014, it is clear that there was an initial 3 day decline at a fairly steep angle (refer to the same chart now edited in image 8). It is therefore necessary to align maybe the second or third grid line from the TT3, with the lows created by this 3 price bar decline. Already we are aware of a fairly savage downward grid developing for this chart but it doesn't necessarily mean that the chart will decline. It does mean however that there will likely be a significant reaction at most if not all of our future grid/overlay lines. It is therefore necessary to take great care at these locations, where price bars are in close proximity to the grid lines. It would be wise to consider placing a stop loss here and this is because the machine that created the grid lines that we are attempting to track, is probably trading 10,000 times bigger than any of us. After approximating the location of the first line, we can begin to gain an insight into the future trend angles which becomes clearer, once we have aligned with the highs of the second downward thrust. These two bold lines have been marked on the top left of image 8 and once these are correctly established, we can predict with a degree of accuracy, the future reaction points (with a little tweaking as new price bars appear.

A second fan has also been projected from the first two solid lines in the centre at the bottom. This time we can use a similar fan for possible break outs higher and for likely forthcoming tripwires, even projecting likely future lines into the white space on the right of the computer monitor. It is important to note at this point that there is usually more than one way to place the TT3 on the chart, simply because the ratios that we are measuring have been imposed by previous activity all over the chart and it is our choice as to which way we can best use them. In Image 8 both fans have been placed in a downward direction which is often the easiest method of locating them because downtrends tend to persist.

IMAGE 8

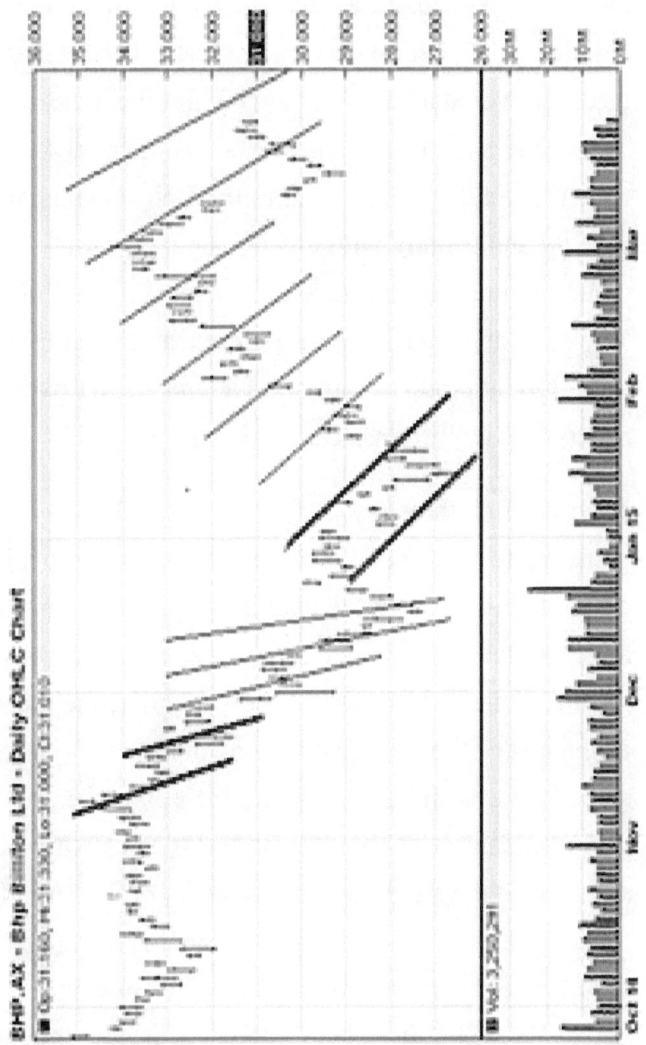

We could have also placed the fans in an upward direction thereby predicting possible future uptrends, but too many grid lines will make the chart more difficult to read. In this case the downtrend is already complete (mid to late December) and with simple inspection it is clear that after those first three price bars from the peak in early November, there are four thrusts lower at a very similar (but not identical angle). This is the basis of our study, that geometry and recurring angles can be used to track financial chart activity and usually with greater accuracy than complimentary tools, such as Fibonacci fans, Elliott Wave, Gann etc. Therefore traders who are familiar with those methods should find Trend and Tripwires not too difficult to master.

After the first three bar decline, the price bars try to consolidate briefly and recover but are then thrust back down the next line in the overlay (suggesting that we have located a trader's grid location). Once these two situations are evident we can now estimate the location of the rest of the TT3 grid. It is also possible to attempt some "Live Trend Tracking" at this point, because the grid is already roughly in place and it can always be adjusted as the chart progresses. More on live trend tracking later in this guide though as this is not an easy skill for beginners to master, it requires practice and perseverance but it yields some very interesting results and inspires great confidence in those with the experience to use it.

If we carefully analyse the angle on the right hand side of this second thrust lower we can now roughly place the grid (EVEN IF THERE WERE NO FURTHER PRICE BARS FOR GUIDANCE)! The lines can hang in white space on the right hand side of the chart. Almost like magic they will react with the price bars when they eventually arrive over the next few days, weeks or months. Still referring to images 7/8 though, we do have further price bars and as the chart progresses we can tweak the initial estimate until ultimately everything aligns with the TT3 guide lines.

At this point I can add a further remarkable discovery to the knowledge base and that is that if the reader can now refer to the complete downtrend from early November to the end of December (where the volume spikes). It is now possible to place an early line from the TT3 overlay to the initial set of lows for this trend and just as in the previous example we can use the second thrust as a guide to place an estimate of the remainder of the grid. So in the same way that we place the tiny segments of the trend, we can also place the larger elements and waves in the trend! In fact because we are dealing with the measurement of pre imposed ratios (ratios that have likely been left by previous computer activity) we can measure intraday, daily weekly, monthly and even annual charts in a similar way.

There is a multitude of different ways to place the TT3 as the pre imposed ratios (derived from a trader's grid), exist everywhere on the chart, it is simply necessary to measure them in a productive way. As we progress I will display multiple charts, as many charts as I feel is necessary to describe the method and to make it as simple and repetitive as possible to apply.

Many people have asked why we cannot include the overlay in software rather than in a laminated A4 sheet and whilst it is of course possible and some charting software companies have attempted this, it is much quicker and easier to spin and align the physical device by taking multiple measurements very quickly and efficiently. As previously mentioned there are many ways to place the overlay depending on your time perspective and it is therefore essential to consider the chart from various angles before a final decision is made. Even then it will usually be necessary to tweak the device slightly as new price bars appear. The user can then photograph the overlay with a smartphone whilst placed on the chart, in order to remember the most significant measurements. The reader is then able to review these phone charts at their leisure, lunch break or whatever.

IMAGE 9

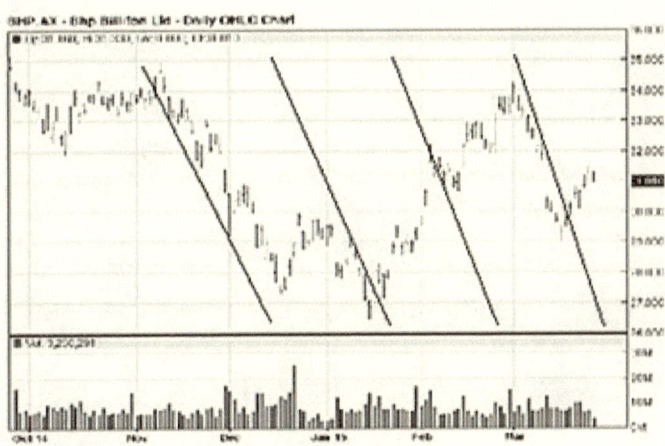

IMAGE 10

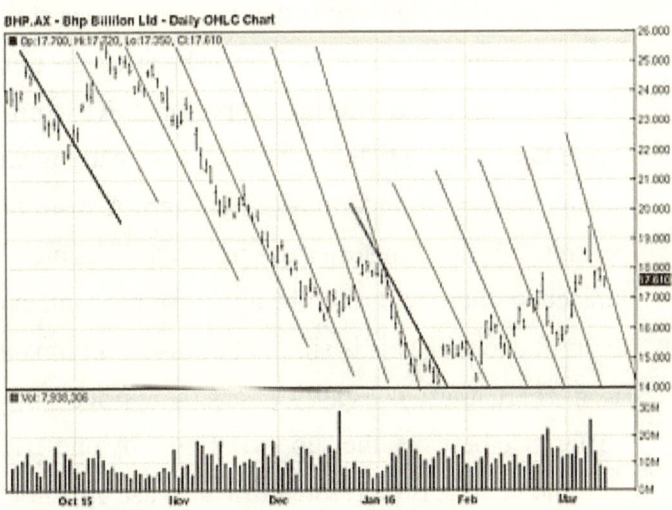

TINY CHARTS

IMAGE 11

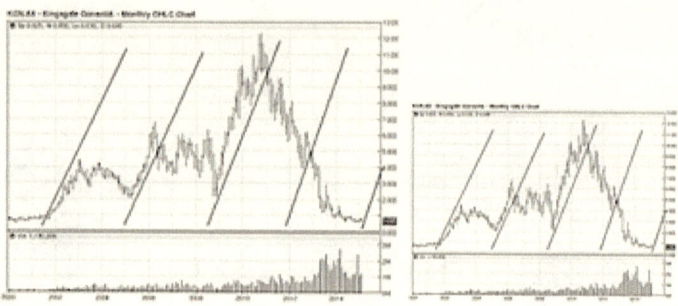

There is a major advantage in tracking longer term tiny charts and the main one is that the trends persist for weeks, months even years. This is because the trend is actually a grid line offering support to newly forming price bars and when this grid line is correctly placed it forms the very foundations of the chart. A word of warning: When longer term foundation lines are breached, there will often be a very significant, even painful decline. This is simply because with longer term charts there is usually a very large price difference between the support offered by one grid line and the next. It is therefore critical to use an automated stop loss strategy in this scenario as a breach of a line could signal a significant decline. However if the grid/trend line holds there is potential for large gains over a significant period. Tiny charts are very informative and inspire confidence, it is almost as if trend or support lines (trends) and resistance lines (tripwires) have been pre-programmed into the chart's future.

It is interesting how accurately the grid lines on the overlay align with existing trends even from five or ten years ago. Elliott wavers and Gann followers are continually warning that some significant chart event is about to occur and without the knowledge and experience gained from analysing many charts over many years, such warnings might be difficult to understand. I suspect that analysts applying these complimentary methods may in fact be commenting on a similar phenomenon to the one that I am describing here, but perhaps simply arriving at a conclusion from a different perspective.

The chart also has to be tiny in order to be fully enclosed by grid lines on the overlay, it is likely that many analysts would miss the opportunities offered by "tiny" charts because mostly we tend to analyse larger charts and probably believe that the larger charts are clearer and offer more possibilities. Sometimes this is not the case and as can be seen in the previous image 11, there have been four very significant uptrends and one possibly developing over the last fifteen years. Ten to fifteen years of chart data is usually sufficient to place at least four grid lines. The more lines that can be confidently placed then the greater the likelihood of cloning the grid on a major trader's computer somewhere. When the lines are correct it should be possible to take one look and see immediately that the grid is clearly influencing the chart. There should be very little doubt and the chart and overlay should appear as one. If there is doubt then the analyst will be less confident of the authority of the lines. There are of course never any guarantees that a trigger point will indeed trigger, but there is a good chance that it will. Furthermore we can use the rising guide line as a stop loss indicator and as can be seen from the chart, it should be treated with great respect. It could be argued that a quick check on the chart to decide if a rising "foundation" trend/line is in place, will reduce some of the risk when trading in a shorter time frame. In other words there is an underlying uptrend supporting good/not so good trading decisions, a kind of safety net in place like when crossing a tight rope. Interestingly a great place to find tiny charts is with a smart phone. They are already tiny enough to use with the overlay, especially for a quick check while at work or sitting in a coffee bar somewhere. I find www.barcharts.com ideal for this (I have no affiliation), as they have an app suitable for tablets and smartphones. There are likely to many suitable alternatives also.

As previously mentioned long term charts in the order of ten to fifteen years, tend to have particularly dominant trend advances/declines that can persist for many months or years and the same TT3 geometry employed to track shorter and medium term charts will easily demonstrate this. Tracking these long term charts requires extraordinary patience and is definitely not suited to a typical day trader. It can take months of waiting to enter a future high probability trend but it is also possible to join an existing trend providing there are some clear navigation points supporting an analyst's view. When the TT3 is ACCURATELY located, the grid line becomes a very useful stop loss and foundation trend line. When the line is breached there is a high probability of a decline and this will be significant on longer term charts, because the price difference between the TT3 lines on multiyear charts can be in the order of dollars and not cents. I tend to prefer to track longer term charts on my smartphone because the charts are TINY and it is much easier to recognise the relationships between the trends. Most of us prefer a huge wide screen monitor or two and this is a great way to focus on the detail in a trend but with the often not considered disadvantage that the relationships between trends are not at all obvious. Everything looks neurotic and random where miniaturisation will prove that it isn't. It is clearly an unfair situation when some insiders are aware of

forthcoming triggers in the data when many other
individuals are not. Perhaps the major players focus on
geometry and the minor players use Fibonacci, Gann,
Elliott or their favourite indicators. Studying the
activity of what appear to be dominant algorithms as
detailed in this book helps to level the playing field a
little. I suspect we are tracking the activity of major
league "algo traders" or "quants" using tell-tale
footprints inadvertently left in the chart by their
software.

MORE TINY CHARTS

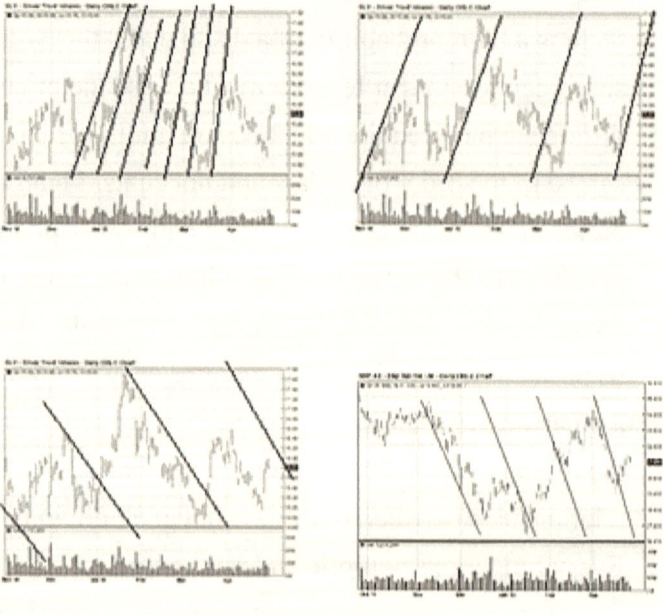

There are many different ways to place the overlay on the chart as the ratios are measurable from many different perspectives. As these ratios between price bars originate from intraday charts, soon they will be evident on daily, weekly and monthly charts. The above tiny charts particularly demonstrate the "Dominant Angles" idea published in the original book. That is that financial trend angles tend to recur over and over and it is now known that this is because the trends are shaped by a grid (which is at least partially represented by our TT3 overlay tool).

In the first Trends and Tripwires book we tracked these with recurring parallels and this is still valid except that now the method can more closely estimate forthcoming trigger points and also even the likely trend angle (which will be relative to previous grid line angles).

I will continue this journey with the study of many bar chart images displaying grid lines traced from the overlay tool (TT3) and the following selection show the clarity and detail that suddenly appears when these grid lines are displayed on the chart. It is like joining the dots in a children's book or wiping the condensation from a window. Suddenly everything is so much clearer, like night and day.

TRY THE TT3 ON THIS TINY CHART

In image 12 a set of down trending TT3 lines has been placed (tripwires). These lines offer a clearer perspective of the chart and identify potential trigger points. Notice that at each TT3 line there is a significant reaction, reinforcing the idea that a grid is indeed in place, aggressively resisting price action at each contact with its lines. Many breaches of these tripwires offer short term potential gain and those with an appetite for the short side of the market will be aware of the "channels" created by pairs of down trending TT3 lines.

IMAGE 12

In image 13 I have retained the tripwires from image 12 but also added an up trending set of TT3 lines (trends). This gives a far clearer impression of the grid that the TT3 was attempting to locate. This grid is quite useful because it displays a part of the underlying geometric structure that is influencing this chart. The chart is no longer random even though it appeared to be at first glance. There is a strong and definite influence underpinning the activity of most financial instruments worldwide and the TT3 demonstrates that this is indeed so.

Just to further complicate matters there is always more than one grid position possible on any chart and careful observation of image 13 will display several recurring short term advances or declines at more extreme angles. Perhaps surprisingly the TT3 can also be located to track these alternative advances. Clearly if all of the possible grid locations were drawn on the chart it would soon become unreadable. It is therefore necessary to choose a grid angle that reflects your style of analysis, passive or aggressive?

IMAGE 13

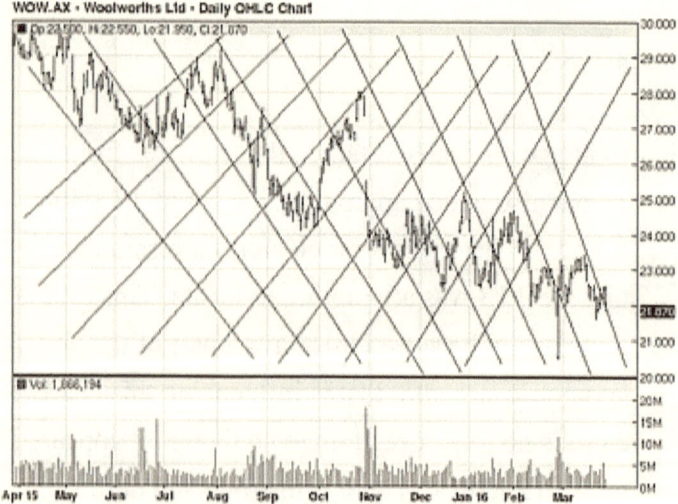

Once the overlay has done its magic the scenario becomes clearer and we can estimate where each segment of the downtrend is likely to retrace (on contact with a down trending tripwire).

IMAGE 14

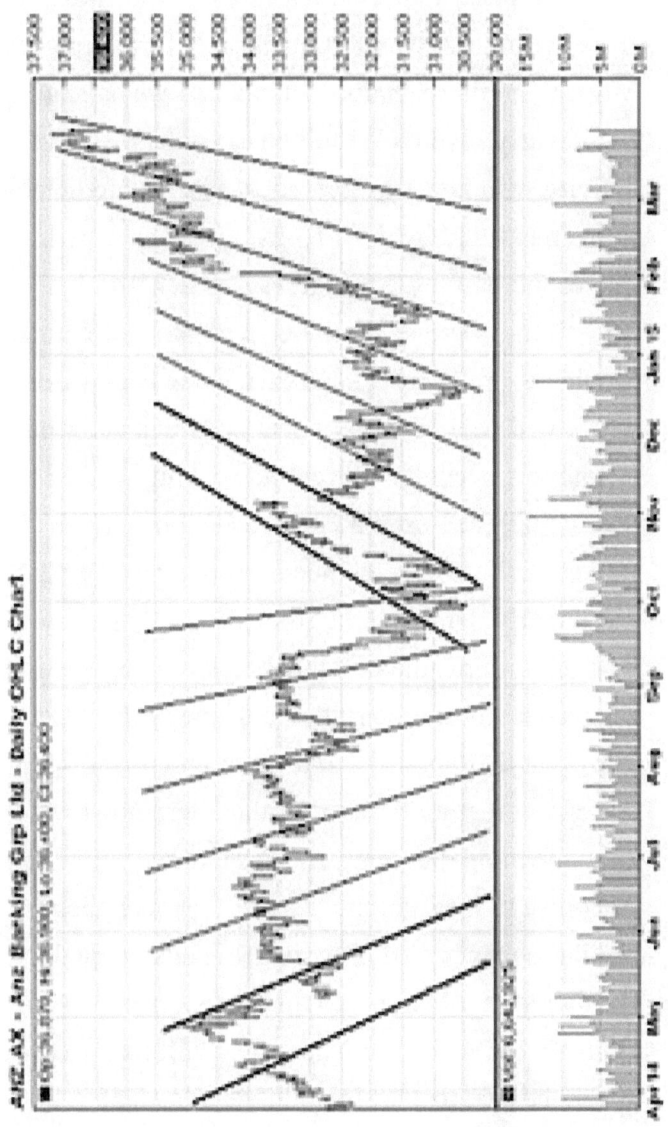

It is clear when these example images are studied, that there appears to be more than one set of grid lines affecting price activity. Images 14 and 15 indicate that there are at least two dominant sets of tripwires influencing these charts. In image 15 we have a particularly severe example that regularly shapes price activity with new tripwires kicking in at predictable ratios measured by the TT3 overlay. The tripwire angles increase by 2.5 degrees for each grid line on the TT3. If this were to continue, eventually of course they would become vertical and then slope backwards. There will be a new set of grid lines in place well before this occurs however and we simply need to take a new reference from a later trend slope. Again in image 15 the new reference lines displayed are not particularly dominant, but they do gently herd price bars and offer some possible break out opportunities. If the reader studies the right hand side of the chart, it is clear that there is still a savage and recurring set of tripwires creating the saw tooth pattern downwards (not drawn on diagram), and the overlay could be used of course to measure the distance between these regular declines also. The reader is encouraged to place the overlay tool on these hair raising examples to estimate each location where they will likely kick in. It would be best to start by tightly enclosing the first narrow downtrend that begins around early to mid-2013 and then project the future tripwires from the overlay. In this case a larger image would be useful because the initial narrow downtrend is not wide enough to align properly with the TT3, whereas usually this method prefers smaller images. Of course with a tablet or smart phone adjusting the size of the image is a trivial matter.

You can either draw TT3 lines with technical analysis software or photograph them with a smartphone. It will be interesting to study the reactions with price bars that will occur at each of the projected grid lines. Just as there are various sets of tripwires, so there are also various sets of trends which we can also track with the TT3 overlay. By analysing the various angles created by obvious runs of price bars, it is possible to be aware of the dominant trends and tripwires within each chart. There are often two or three examples vying for dominance within each chart and it is our job to locate those that dominate overall.

IMAGE 15

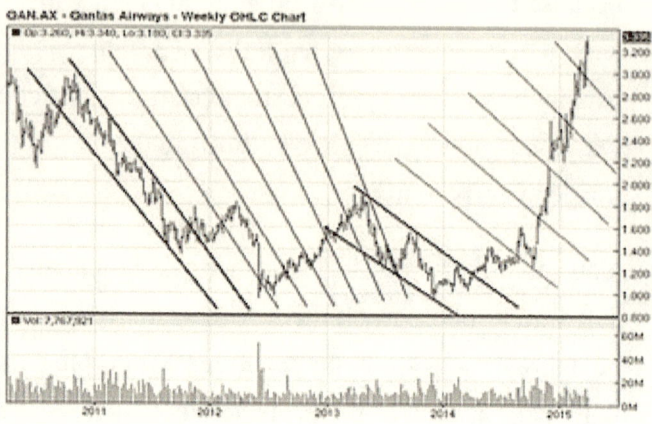

IMAGE 16

Some of the extreme trend triggers in the SLV chart (image 16) would have been rewarding for those with the patience to wait for them and the confidence to trust the overlay signal when it arrived. On a weekly or monthly chart the distance between the low and high is often in the order of several dollars, in this case there were three examples where the price change was around ten dollars and certainly worth waiting for. As previously stated there is more than one possible location to place the overlay but usually enclosing the segment between the solid lines is a fairly reliable place to start. The FIRST solid line can align with the highs of the rising price bars BUT it can also just pivot on the highest high as shown in image 16 around early 2011. The angle of the SECOND solid line will very often provide the best clue as to the location of the rest of the grid that appears to be dominating chart activity. In image 16 on the far left initial uptrend it is clear that after placing the first two or three lines, analysts could be fairly confident of the angle and location of the forthcoming rising trend lines. At the fifth rising line however the trigger didn't happen and as this is a weekly chart with significant potential price gains and losses close to the grid lines, a close stop loss would be crucial.

IMAGE 17

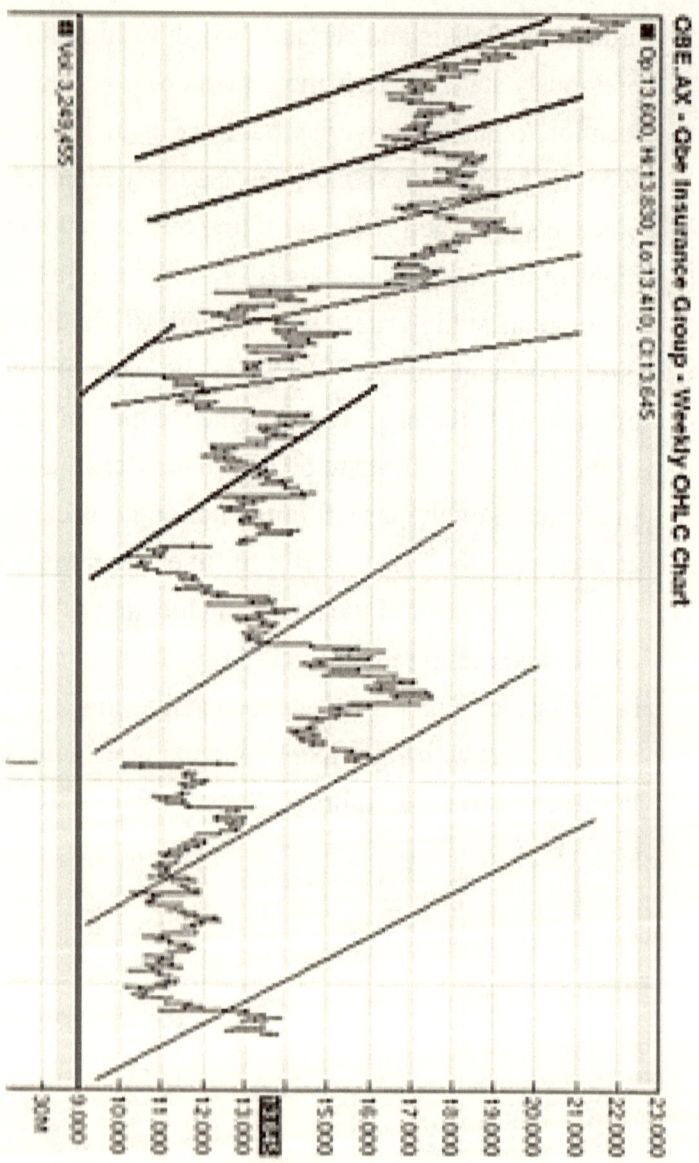

IMAGE 18 – SILVER ITRUST

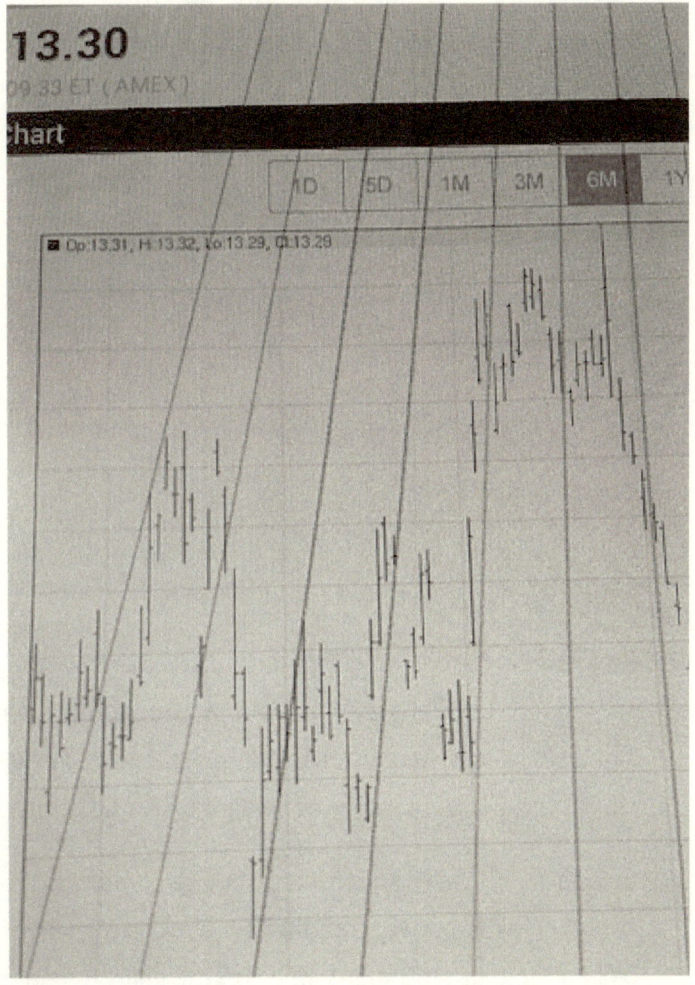

If the user had correctly aligned the first two or three grid lines from the TT3 on image 18 the silver chart represented by ITRUST, then the next two projected grid lines offered some interesting opportunities.

Notice that after the fifth rising grid line, the sixth and seventh are back sloping offering no further opportunity until the TT3 is repositioned.

IMAGE 19

Image 19 offered some regularly spaced advances on this longer term chart. Great patience is required when analysing these longer term examples and moves up or down can be in the order of dollars instead of cents.

Image 20 displays an uprising set of trend or grid lines together with a down trending set of possible tripwires. When there are too many lines on the chart the analysis can become too complicated but this is an interesting visualisation of some of the opposing forces at play on any given chart. Even on this ten year chart the grid lines are influencing price activity quite considerably.

IMAGE 20

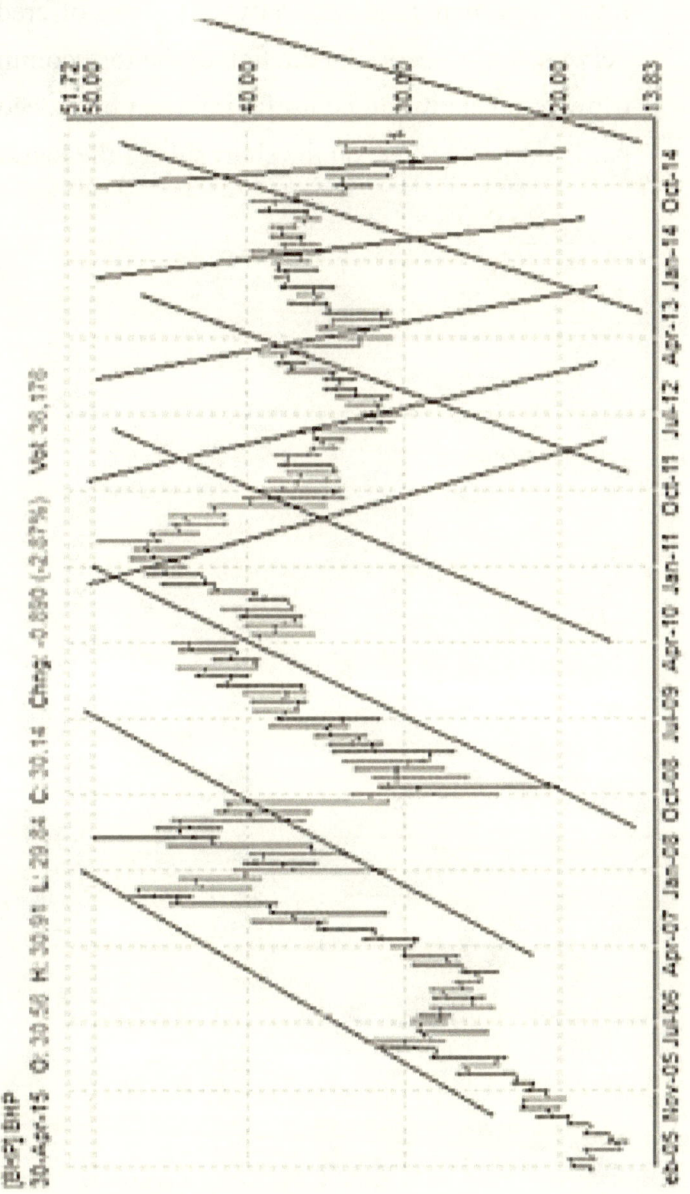

In image 21 we can see that carefully enclosing the first clear down trend within two TT3 lines offered a very useful projection/prediction of the forthcoming tripwires. This would be useful information indeed particularly for those on the short side of the market.

IMAGE 21

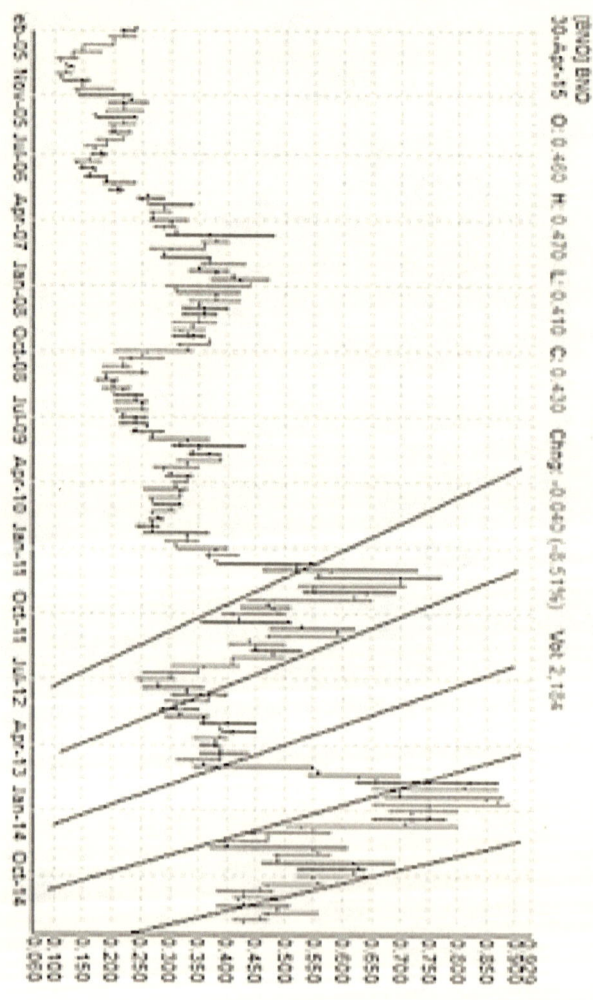

IMAGE 22

Image 22 has been aligned a little differently than image 21 but the lines are still valid. The ratio measurements provided by the TT3 are evident all over the chart and probably assist trading computers by providing predictable trigger points. Computers are more reliable of course when operating in a controlled and predictable environment.

IMAGE 23

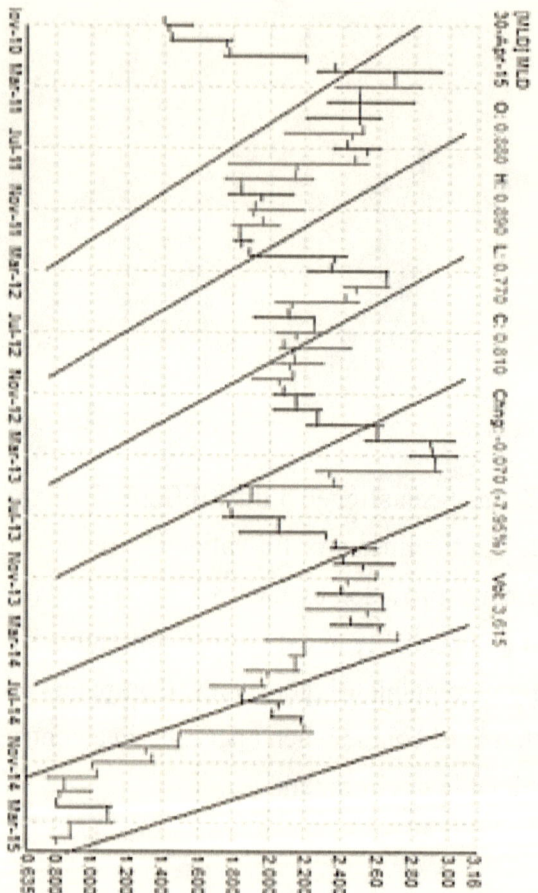

Image 23 has again been enclosed by TT3 lines offering a degree of predictability for future activity. As a trend progresses it is often necessary to widen the TT3 by sliding it down to make the gaps a little wider. This is to compensate for the fact that we do not know the exact scale of the chart and increases the accuracy of future signals.

IMAGE 24

Image 24 is an image from a tablet computer that has been photographed with a smart phone. This offers a quick and convenient method for saving interesting charts for analysis. This chart appears to be approaching a tripwire or perhaps a possible breakout opportunity.

IMAGE 25

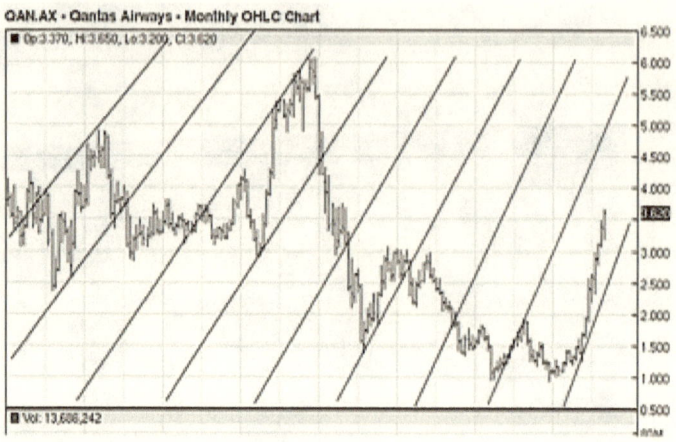

QAN.AX • Qantas Airways • Monthly OHLC Chart

FOUNDATION TRENDS

Longer term trends and tripwires tend to persist and their influence is evident at regular intervals on the next few 10 year charts. I call these foundation trends because they underpin the trend direction and give a strong signal that momentum is weakening when the current line is broken. These longer term trends can persist for many months and provided they are supported by an accurate TT3 line, the user can feel confident of the trend. The TT3 can be placed on a long term chart in exactly the same way that it is placed on an intra-day or daily chart etc. The ratios between trends have already been imposed on the price bars probably by an external computer and they can therefore be measured with the overlay tool.

IMAGE 26

Image 26 offered some excellent signals on this 10 year chart, the tripwires were quite savage and the TT3 located them well in advance of forthcoming activity by carefully locating the first three grid lines.

IMAGE 27

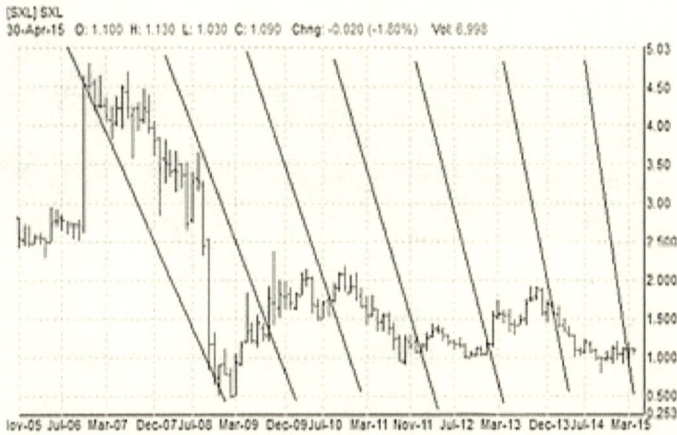

IMAGE 28

Image 28 is a six month chart with very accurately placed tripwires which may have offered some interesting opportunities.

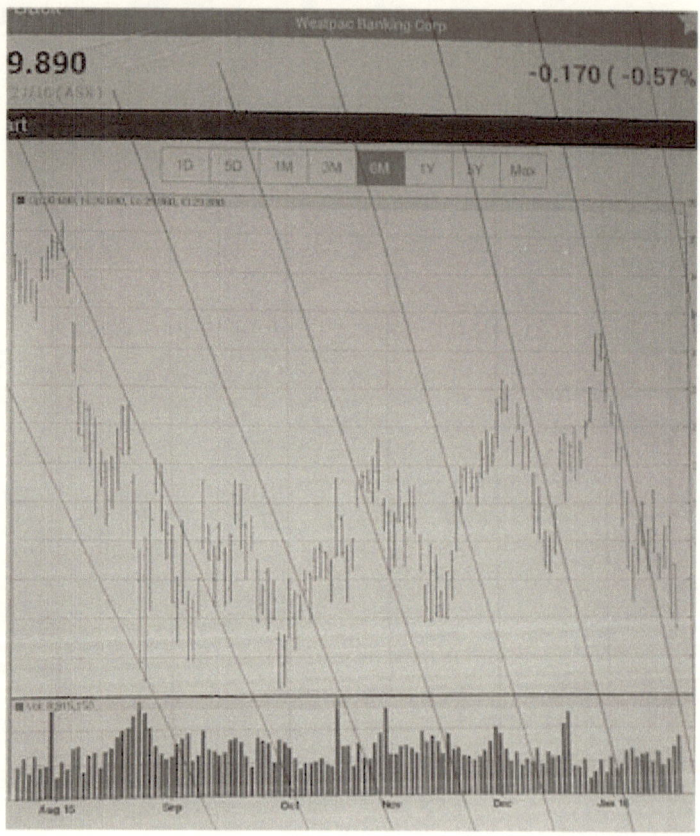

IMAGE 29

It should be becoming clear by now that smaller charts hold the key to recognising hidden relationships in trends. When we buy the latest wide screen monitor the price bars are certainly clearer but our perception of the chart will change completely. Imagine zooming right in to a street in mapping software, seeing it entirely in isolation and being entirely unaware of its location relative to the nearest highway, freeway etc. This is the kind of situation we find ourselves in when using a huge monitor. In many ways it is better to go smaller and this is where smartphones and tablet computers become indispensable. This may seem counter intuitive as many people are guilty of buying the biggest believing it to be the best, but at least with this method of technical analysis this is not always the

75

case. In the previous few images 26, 27 and 29 the TT3 grid lines have been placed on 10 year charts and I tend to think of these as "Foundation Trends." It is clear from these charts that either a trend or a tripwire will tend to recur at regular intervals and with the potential to make or break your year. These are I believe the key to trading with the trend, if your position is supported by a foundation trend there is a greater chance that it will persist for some time to come. These provide the analyst with a foundation for the chart, a kind of backbone that offers strength to a trend simply because it represents a very significant long term grid line, borrowed from some major league trader's chart somewhere.

SMARTPHONE AND TABLET

There is quite an advantage to be gained in placing the overlay carefully on a bar chart displayed on a tablet computer, mainly due to their compact size and portability. The next step is to take a smartphone and photograph the image which now includes the price bars combined with the grid lines from the overlay, (much like the many example images on the following pages). Be careful to ensure that the price bars line up with the overlay lines, as it is easy to distort the image by taking the photo at an odd angle, which sometimes gives the impression that the grid lines are not touching the price bars when they actually are. It is a quick and convenient method when mastered, it also saves drawing the trends and tripwires manually and allows the user to carry charts in the phone's memory to check at a spare moment's notice. When the lines are properly drawn, the user will feel confident that they are correct because the grid lines now seem to be an integral part of the image. If there is reasonable doubt then the grid lines are probably not correctly placed. The overlay and the price bars should seem like two pieces of the same puzzle with a seamless connection. The following selection of images has been created by using a smartphone to photograph my (Galaxy) tablet computer. It is wise to study these images very closely to thoroughly understand how the overlay has been placed. By this stage of the book the reader should be fairly well acquainted with the approach, but there is always room to learn. It really doesn't matter which company we are tracking because as previously stated, the method is generic and therefore applicable to almost any liquid financial chart worldwide. Most of these examples are taken from ASX charts with a major USA index or two thrown in.

The author has analysed literally thousands of charts from all over the world including shares, currencies, commodities etc. and so far the only anomalies I have found are (thinly traded) non liquid examples. Even these charts can be correctly analysed when using weekly or monthly charts as the volume is greater and price bars are fully formed. Heavily traded high volume charts are the most suitable for analysis with this method as we require each price bar to be fully formed to take full advantage of the analysis tool.

Note that in the following chart (image 30), that the overlay has been placed on the first significant breakout. The overlay will seem to "predict" the following "trend" lines after the first two have been correctly placed, but really it is simply indicating the spacing for the rest of the vertical grid lines. Usefully it will indicate where likely rallies or trigger points may occur (no guarantees of course).

Perhaps even more usefully it can also predict likely forthcoming tripwires and these down trending grid lines are particularly reliable and tend to persist. This may be due to professional short selling as it is possible to trade both the trends and the tripwires when armed with sufficient knowledge.

SMARTPHONE AND TABLET CHARTS

IMAGE 30

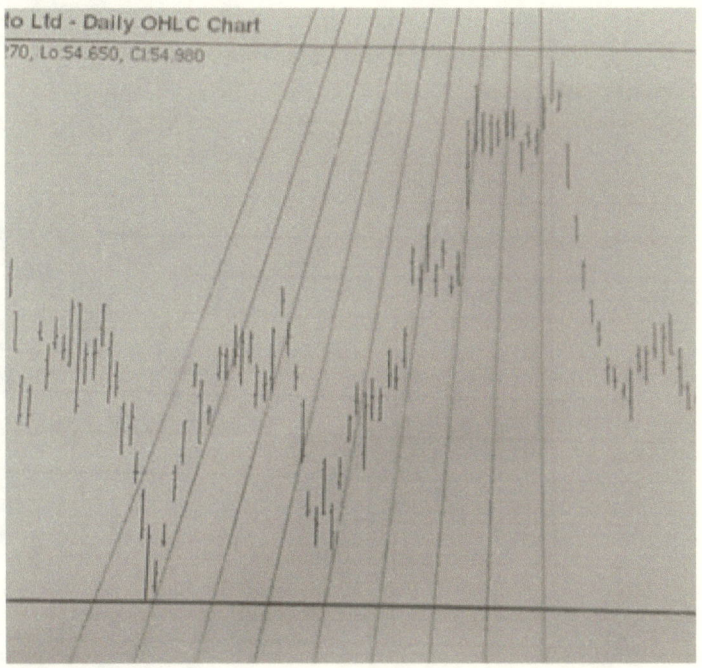

The additional lines on the new TT3 provide greater detail to the trend activity and also assist the analyst in placing trend/grid lines with greater confidence. It is interesting to note with image 30, that the triggers were quite reliable on contact with each grid line, but when the far right grid line failed to trigger price bars fell decisively for several days.

IMAGE 31

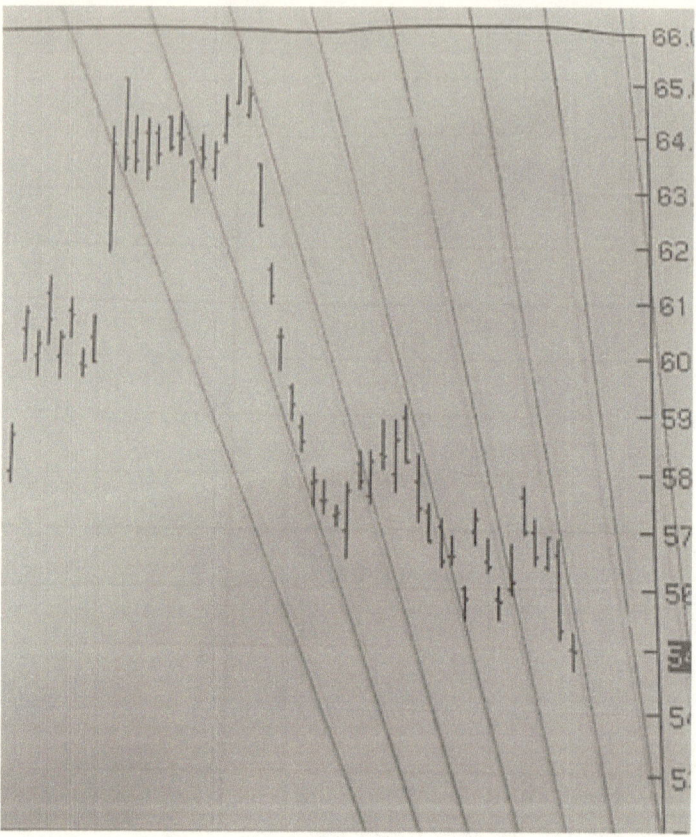

The second and third grid lines have been carefully located above in image 31 and after the first and fourth lines have been tweaked to fit we can fairly reliably locate the rest of the hidden grid. When the likely rally points are plotted on the same chart as the previous example, it is clear that at this stage sellers are very much in control and any rallies are short lived or nonexistent. In reality this chart would have been one of the more difficult charts to track.

Sometimes it is more sensible to find another one with a greater degree of predictability and this depends on your level of confidence with the location of the grid.

IMAGE 32

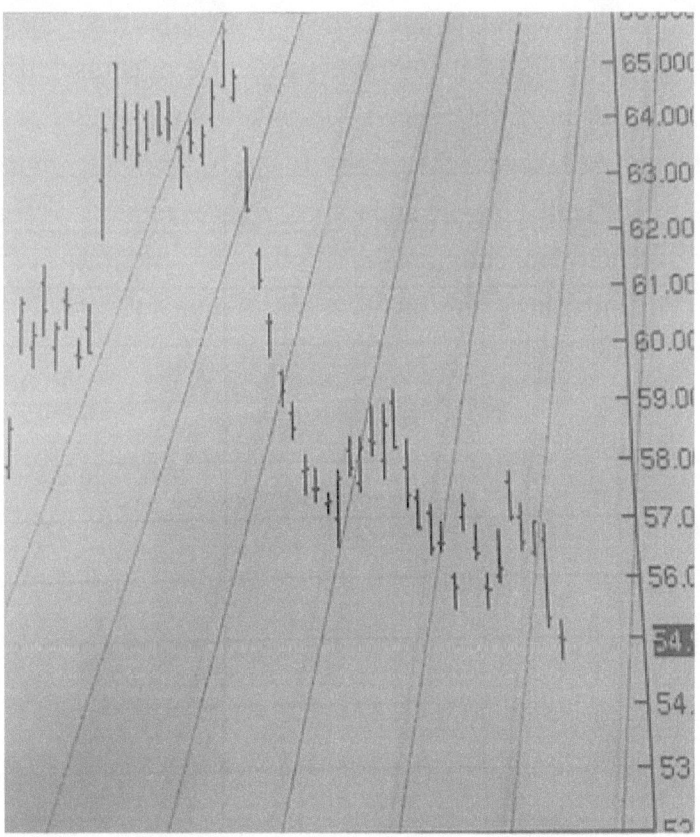

Sometimes it is best to align the HIGHS in the initial breakout with the first grid line and sometimes the LOWS work better and both may be valid. The trick is to tweak the overlay position until it is reliably revealing the likely rally points. This is why the TT3 overlay (the newest overlay tool at the time of writing), has additional analysis lines. It is because the extra lines can be stepped back in time by moving the whole grid one or two lines to the left. Using earlier rally/reaction points in the data helps users to "predict" future lines with more accuracy. It is of course difficult to achieve 100% accuracy but the closer to that goal then the better the results. Image 32 is another more difficult example and the wise trader might look for a chart with additional reactions at the grid lines before committing, this one is too risky in my opinion.

IMAGE 33

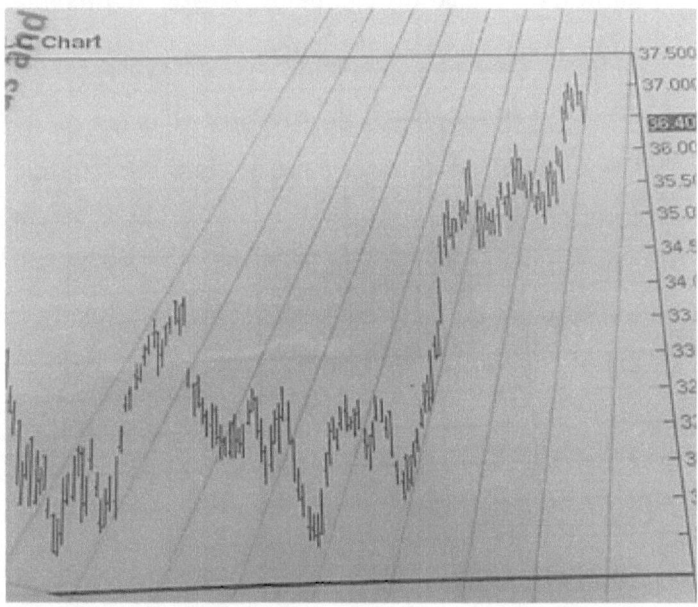

Image 33 might have inspired more confidence because when the first three or four lines have been located we can be fairly confident of the location of the rest of the grid. This chart offered some outstanding possibilities.

The chart in image 34 (and also 33) is a good example of the significant advantage that can be gained by the use of the extra lines in the TT3 overlay tool.

It is clear that by carefully enclosing the first downward thrust with the first two overlay lines in image 34, we are better able to "predict" the locations of the following tripwires. Break outs often occur when a tripwire is finally breached. Several potential short term breakouts can be recognized in this image and a few dangerous tripwires.

It is wise to remember that the analyst is not really "predicting" anything, we are not looking into the future in any kind of manner proposed by Einstein. The earlier grid lines simply reveal the probable locations of the later examples. The grid already exists and it is up to the analyst to try and locate it.

IMAGE 34

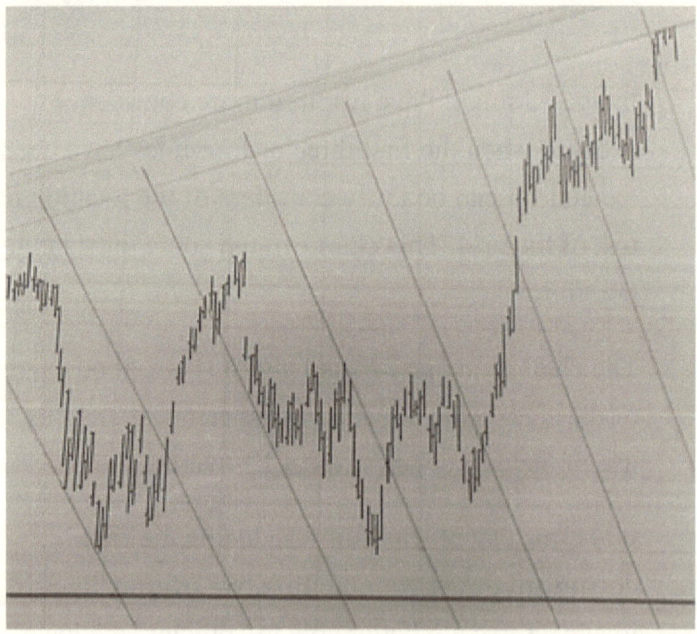

Each of these smartphone images offers an insight into the accurate use of the TT3 overlay tool. The reader will hopefully come to appreciate that every chart can be analysed much more accurately than with many other more conventional approaches. It would be interesting for an Elliott Wave, Gann or Fibonacci analyst to incorporate trends and tripwires into their current approach to further develop an arsenal of formidable analysis tools.

The TT3 is available at www.trendsandtripwires.com

IMAGE 35

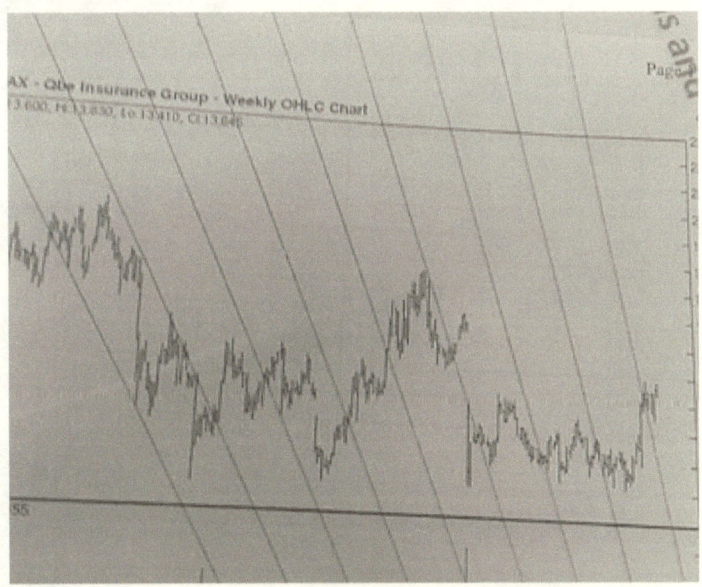

Whilst the gap down would have been more than a little unsettling on the next chart in image 36, some of the following opportunities had some potential. On a weekly or monthly chart there is more time to plan and analyse, but you certainly need patience and the moves are much larger, both up and down.

IMAGE 36

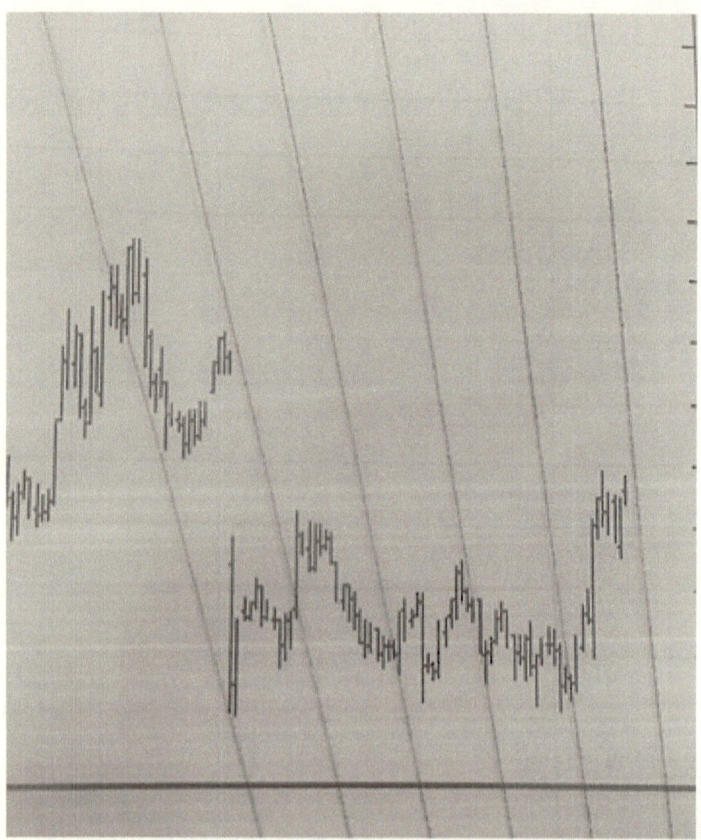

Notice the reactions at each tripwire on the grid and exercise caution as the chart is approaching another.

Both the trends (up) and tripwires (down) can be plotted and analysed using the TT3 overlay tool offering the potential for persistent gain on weekly or monthly charts depending on whether the analyst prefers the long or short side of the market. The overlay simultaneously measures slices of price and time, a two dimensional analysis on a typical chart and in a fast, simple and convenient way.

IMAGE 37

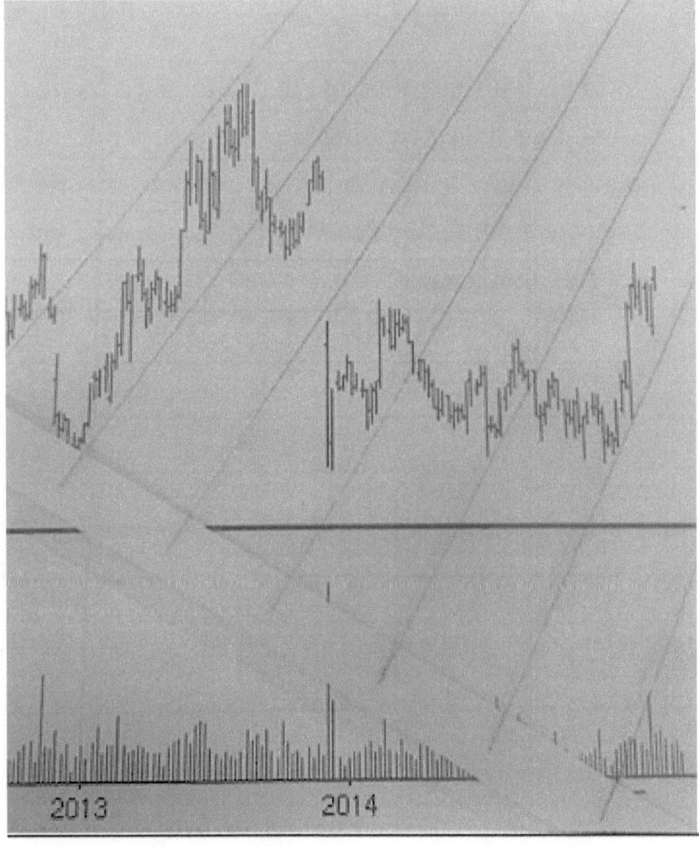

The grid lines on image 37 have indicated likely support trends quite well so far offering a degree of comfort to an analyst. If the overlay were to be rotated anti-clockwise a little it would assist in locating the recurring even steeper trends that are evident on this chart.

These smartphone/tablet charts are real world images of the TT3 overlay as applied to liquid financial charts. When two or preferably three grid lines are accurately placed, then the user can begin to feel confident that the locations of likely future triggers have been located. It is quite possible that automated trading computers are calculating these trigger points and placing trades here with fairly tight stops. In effect they are continually throwing mud at the wall knowing for sure that some of it will stick. For them it is a numbers game, a disciplined systematic approach should pay dividends.

DOW U.S. INDICES - (TRENDS AND TRIPWIRES)

IMAGE 38

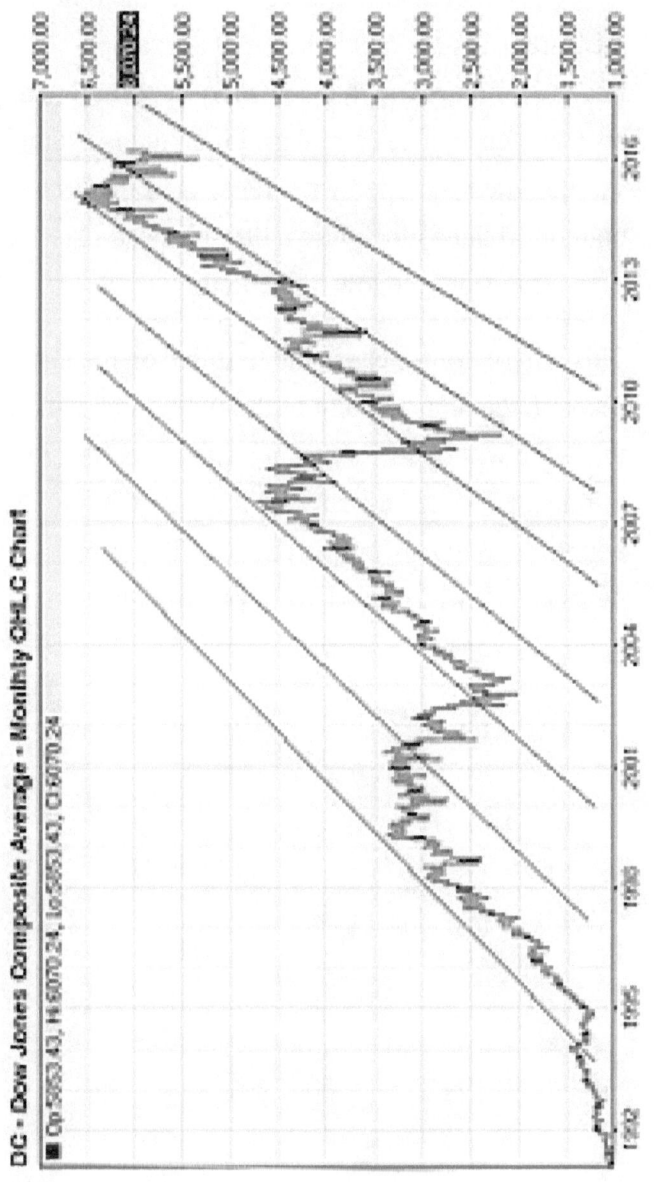

IMAGE 39 – DOW 25 YEAR CHART

Some indices are a little more difficult to track and the major US indices are no exception but the ratio measurements are quite clear in this example with image 39 suggesting that a primary support line has been breached. The central grid line in this example should now be aligned with the lows of the central uptrend (rotated clockwise a little) instead of skewering from the low to the high.

This will of course cause the first line on the left to pivot on the highest point of the first uptrend and the third line will be lower and at a shallower angle ready to find a possible new support level for the now tumbling price bars on the far right. It will be necessary to widen the TT3 lines a little by sliding it upwards.

$INDU - DOW Industrials [Test] - Monthly OHLC Chart

IMAGE 40

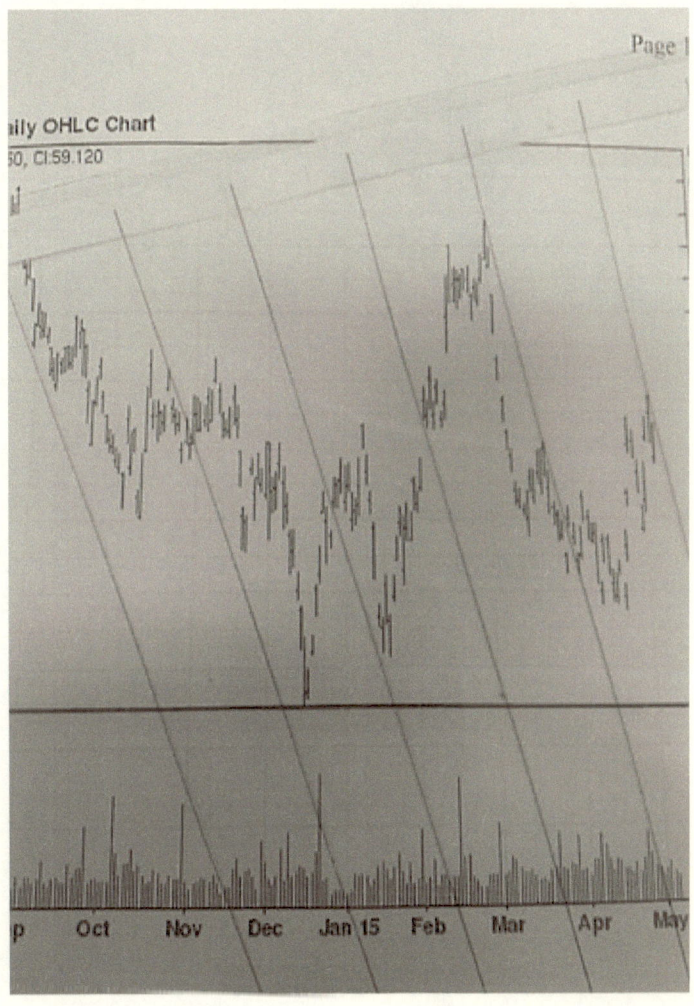

IMAGE 41

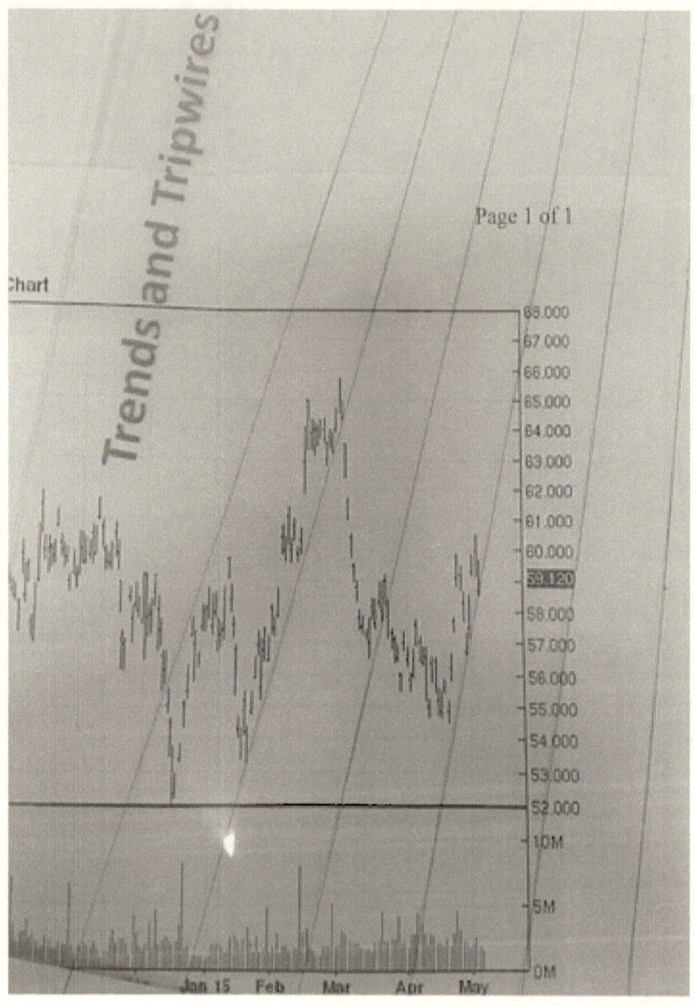

IMAGE 42

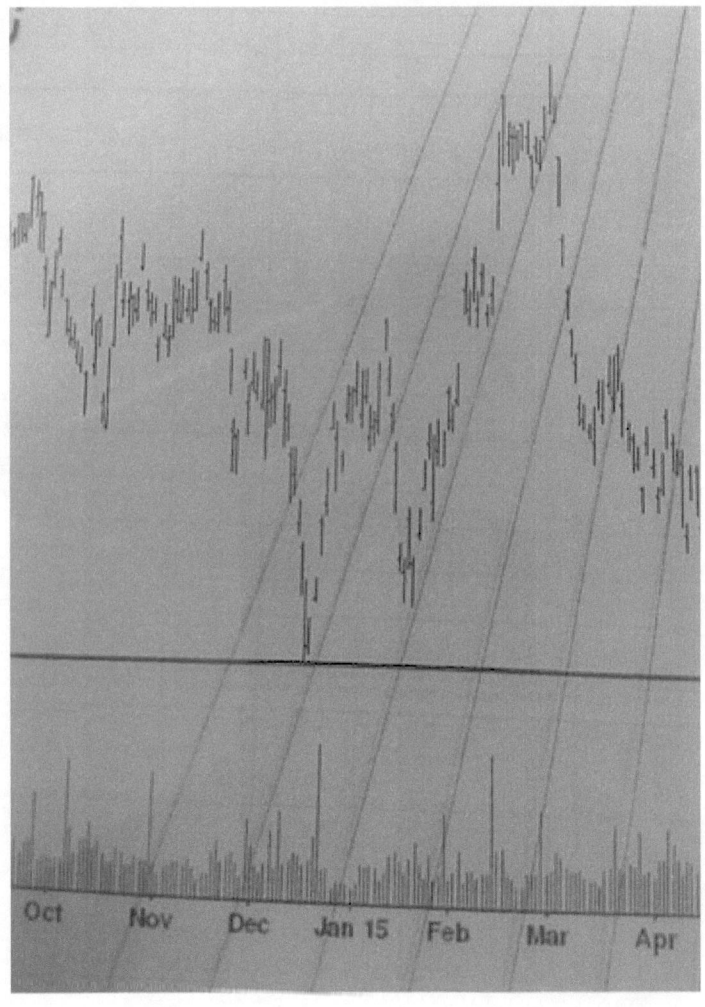

IMAGE 43

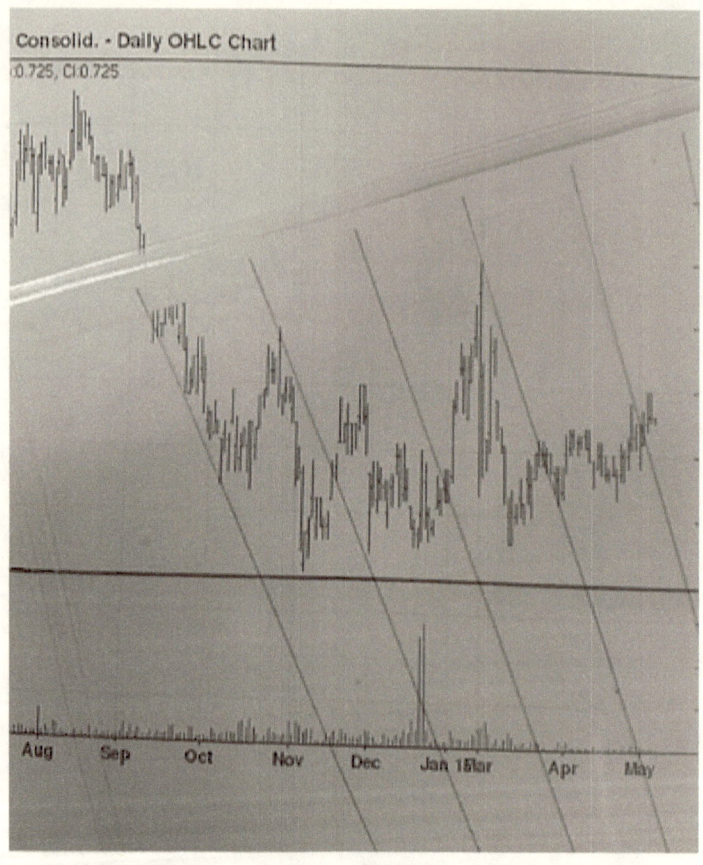

IMAGE 44

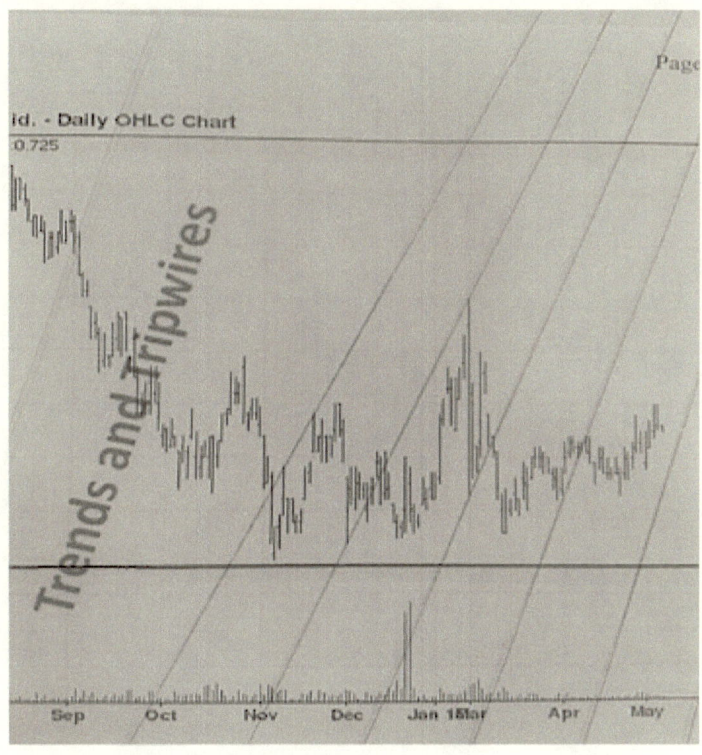

IMAGE 45

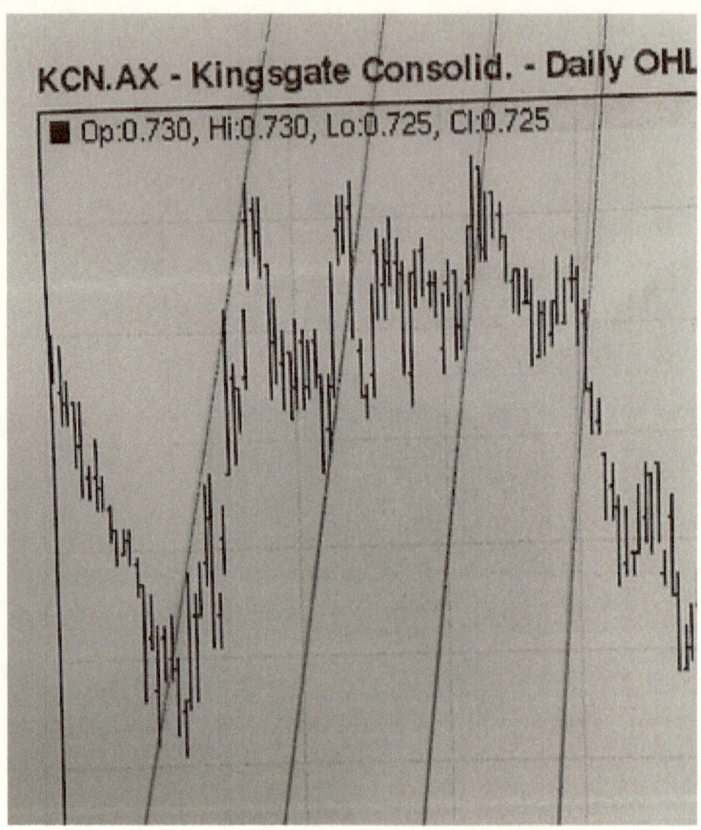

IMAGE 46

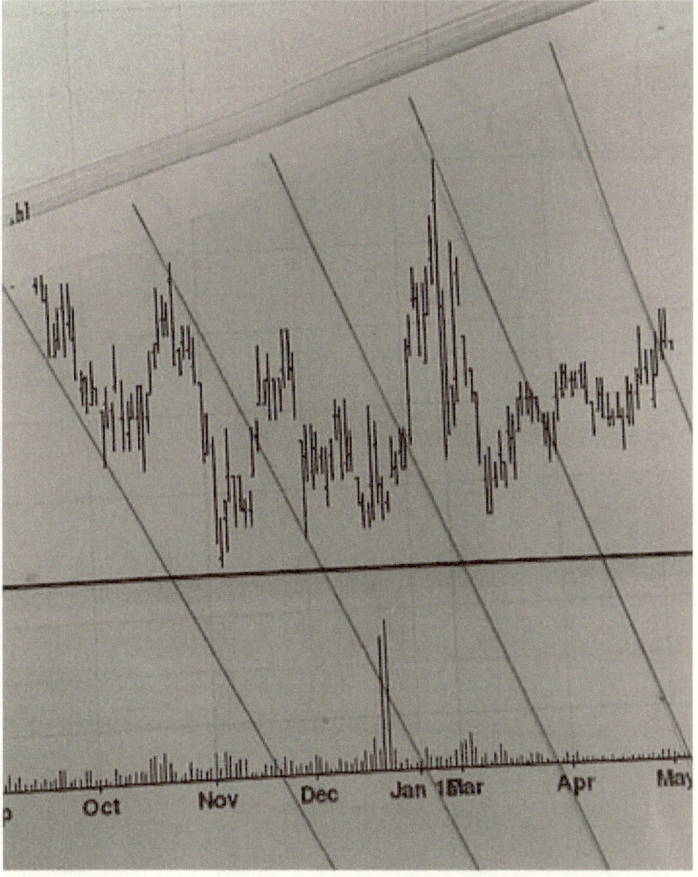

Images 46, 47 and 48 are all from the same chart but analysed from different perspectives, with chart 46 and 48 displaying likely tripwires and chart 47 some of the potential trends and support lines. Of course it is possible to trade both sides of the market and these charts show how the overlay can help to guide an analyst's decision making.

IMAGE 47

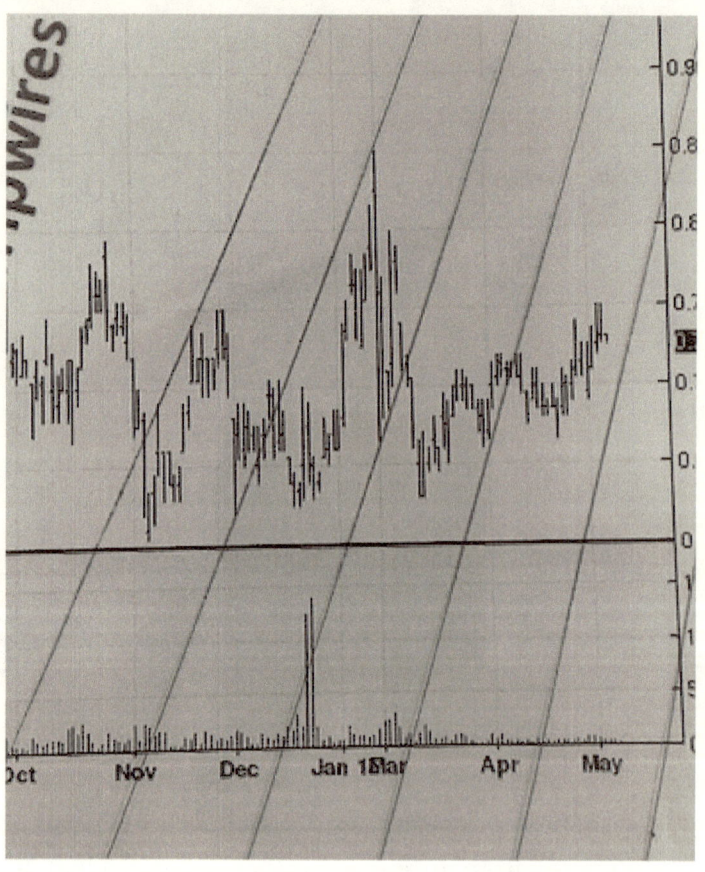

When carefully considered, charts 46, 47 and 48 suggest likely trigger points for potential trends and tripwires on shorter term charts, they also offer a useful estimation of likely price targets.

IMAGE 48

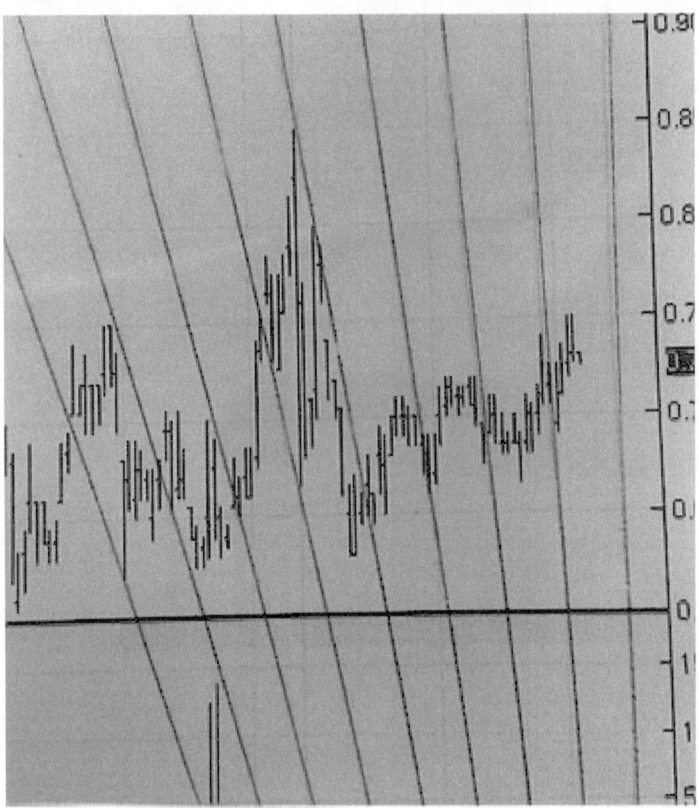

Image 48 has been more tightly enclosed with tripwires and reveals interesting break out or trigger points and likely price targets. These shorter term examples require a much higher level of attention.

IMAGE 49 – RIO DAILY CHART

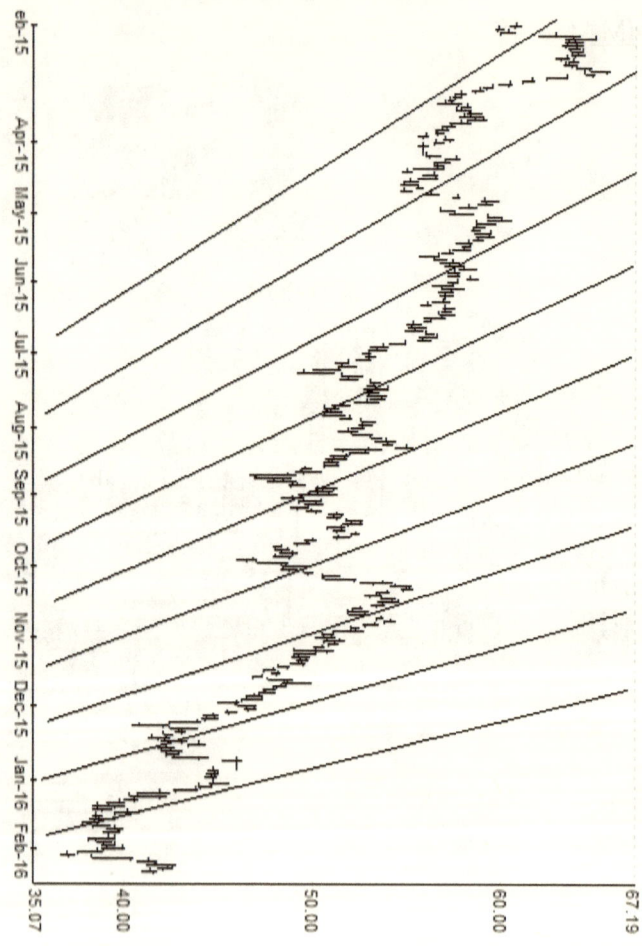

IMAGE 50 – CALTEX DAILY CHART

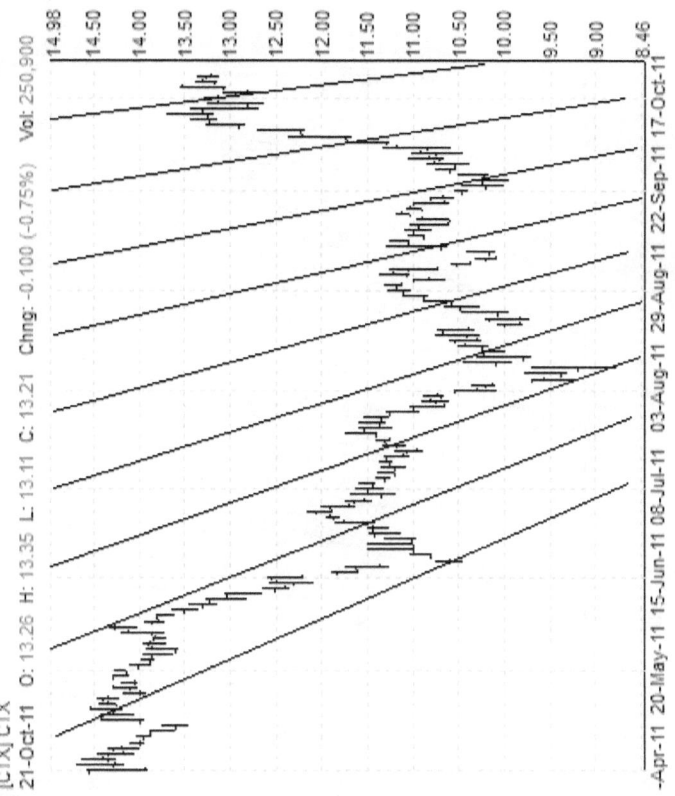

IMAGE 51 – WESFARMERS 6 MONTHS

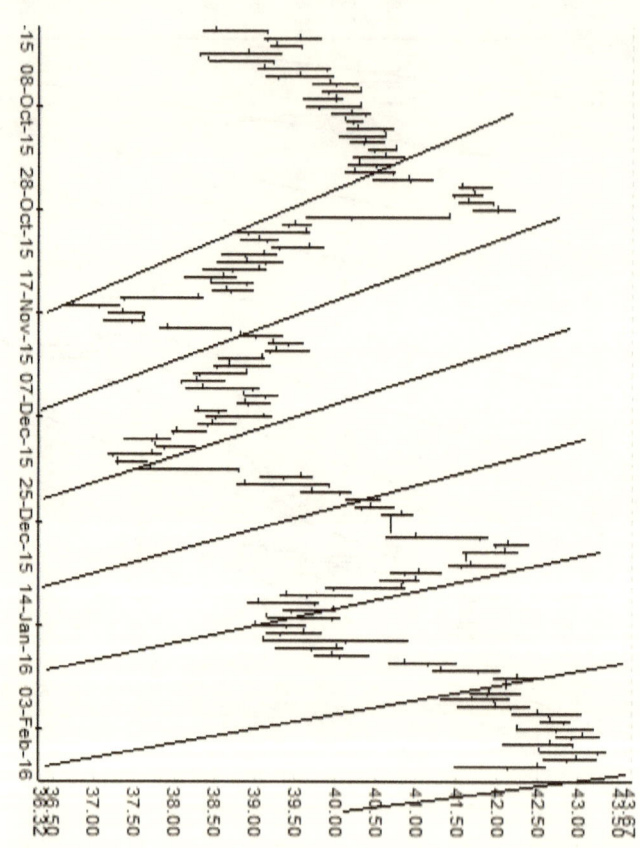

IMAGE 52 – WESFARMERS 12 MONTHS

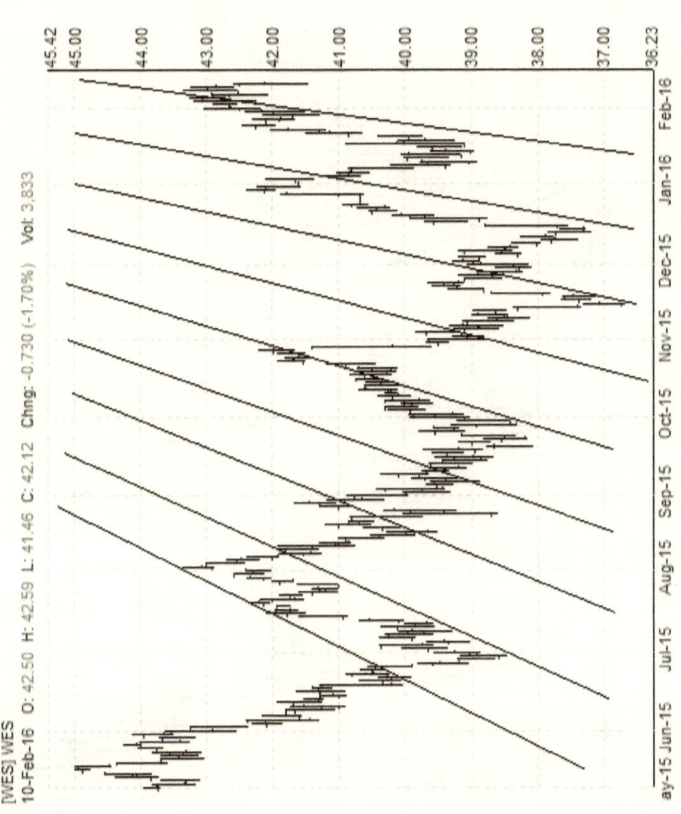

IMAGE 53 – WESFARMERS STEEP TRENDS

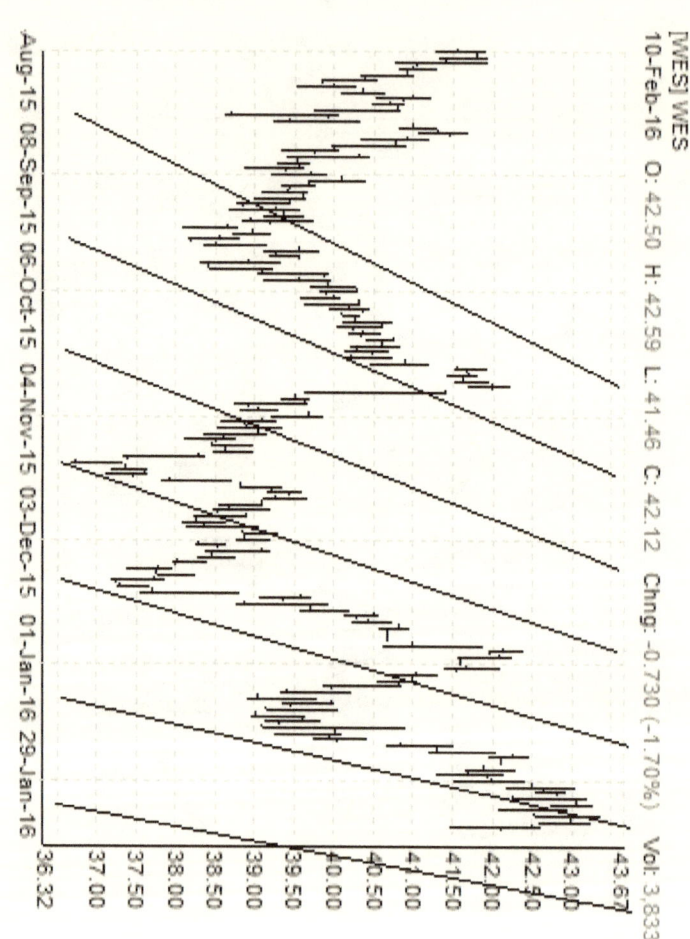

IMAGE 54 – WESFARMERS 12 MONTHS

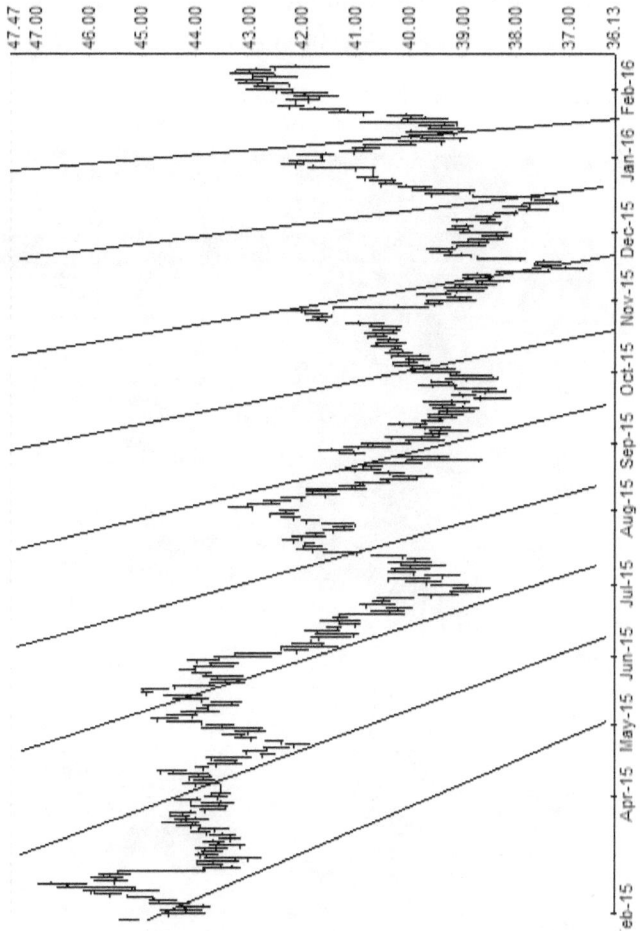

Images 51 – 54 (all of Wesfarmers for no particular reason), illustrate that the TT3 can turn apparently random and chaotic charts into something with order, structure and a degree of predictability.

IMAGE 55 E-MINI S&P 500 (left hand side)

It is quite remarkable viewing the obvious grid influence on images 55 and 56 which has been revealed by the TT3 overlay.

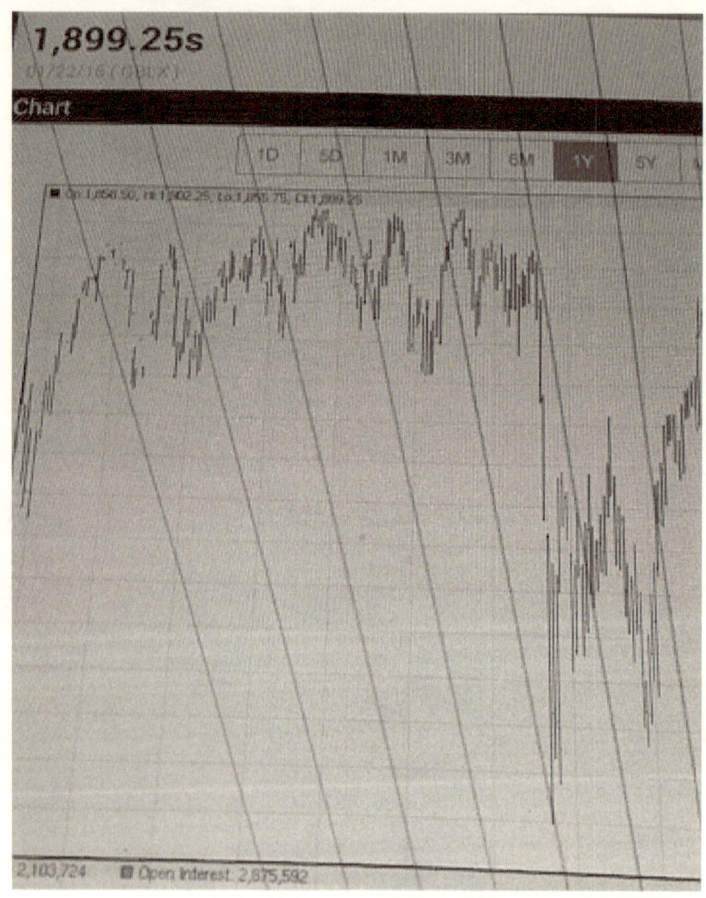

IMAGE 56 E-MINI S&P 500 – (right hand side)

On image 56 the TT3 has been repositioned to reveal the influence of the grid on the right hand side of this 12 month E-MINI S&P 500 chart. An analyst would likely place the TT3 as in image 55 and as the activity develops the TT3 would be relocated as in image 56.

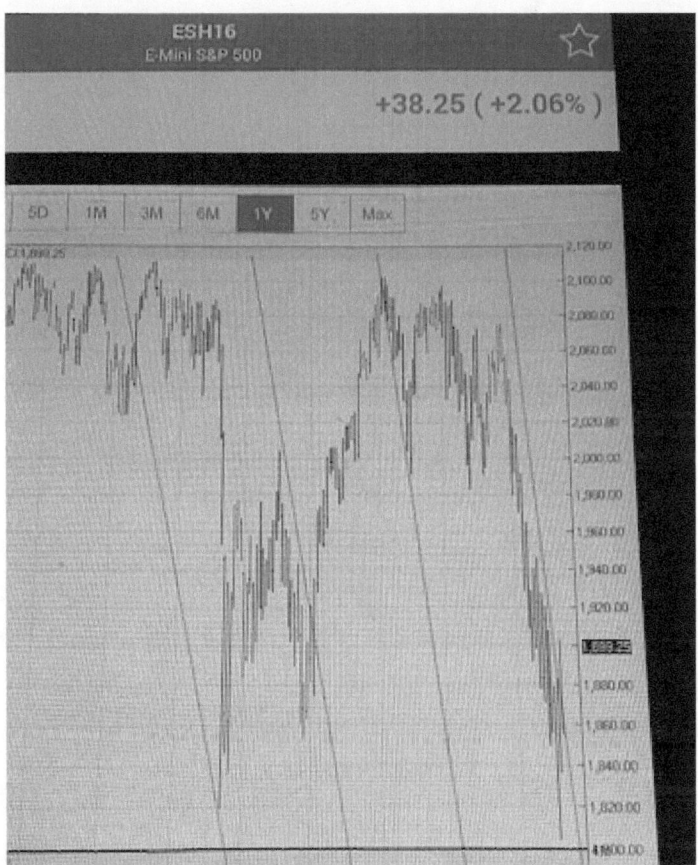

IMAGE 57 AMP DAILY

AMP.AX - Amp Ltd - Daily OHLC Chart
Op 5.720, Hi 5.790, Lo 5.695, Cl 5.730

LIVE TREND TRACKING

Using the TT3 in a real time environment is both interesting and educational and perhaps the best example of this would be with a one minute tick chart (it will still work fine with (5,10, 20 or 30 minutes etc). The TT3 lines when placed correctly will react with the price bars on contact giving the analyst confidence that our grid lines are replicating those at the top end of the market. Observing the activity in real time is very satisfying and because new price bars are forming every minute, (or fifteen or thirty or whatever), it doesn't take long to appreciate the extent of the grid's influence in all major markets. The method is as described for most other charts within these pages.

The user should enclose a very recent completed trend within two TT3 lines paying particular emphasis to the SECOND line and its angles or slope. When an angle/slope has been located correctly the user should preferably wait for the next corner or reaction in the trend and align the third TT3 line. Often it is necessary to slide the tool a little to make the lines wider. Now the user should watch and wait for reactions at the next few lines of the grid. It is useful with intraday charts to display two or three days of fully formed price bars (not dashes) as this will indicate how one day is connected to the next.

Another useful method for practising live trend tracking is to use historical charts. The user should display preferably around 100-200 price bars in any time scale on a smartphone or tablet. If the chart is displayed on a computer then reduce the size of the chart to about 30 % of its full size. This will ensure that the TT3 lines work properly with the image. Now cover the chart with a blank sheet of paper ensuring that the image is completely obscured. Now with only the leftmost side of the chart visible, the reader can place their TT3 and estimate the position of the dominant grid that is driving price activity. As the sheet of paper is very slowly moved to the right, the overlay can be adjusted a little and widened to fit the first breakout slope emerging and maybe two or three peaks and valleys. From this point the paper can be dragged further across the chart to watch the "future" price bars run up and down the TT3 lines. It may still be necessary to adjust its location as the price bars emerge into view. After practising the technique on many charts, the reader can use the TT3 in the opposite direction with the apex at the bottom. The overlay should be aligned with the first downward break and adjusted when new peaks and valleys emerge just as in the many example images in this book. This exercise will give the user greater confidence in the use of the overlay tool and perhaps finally convince you that the market is not at all as random as it appears to be.

Just before moving on to the conclusion of this book, I have provided images 58 and 59 to illustrate how charts of different time scales are related. It is simply a matter of detail, as a weekly chart is a compressed version of a daily chart and a monthly chart is a compressed version of a weekly chart and so on. What this means is that a five day week is consolidated into a single weekly price bar and roughly four working weeks becomes a single monthly price bar. So looking at images 58 and 59 it is clear that a similar TT3 shape location applies to both charts. The difference is that the weekly chart has much less detail because obviously there are far fewer price bars used in its construction (5:1). A similar principle applies with daily to intraday charts, a similar TT3 location will still apply to both but there is more or less detail between them. This presents readers with one reason why the TT3 can be applied to intraday, daily, weekly charts etc. A good example of this idea can be found in FCharts pro technical analysis software where it is a simple matter to switch between daily, weekly views etc. This remarkable program is available surprisingly inexpensively from www.spacejock.com

Many of the charts in this publication are included courtesy of Spacejock software.

IMAGE 58 - DAILY CHART

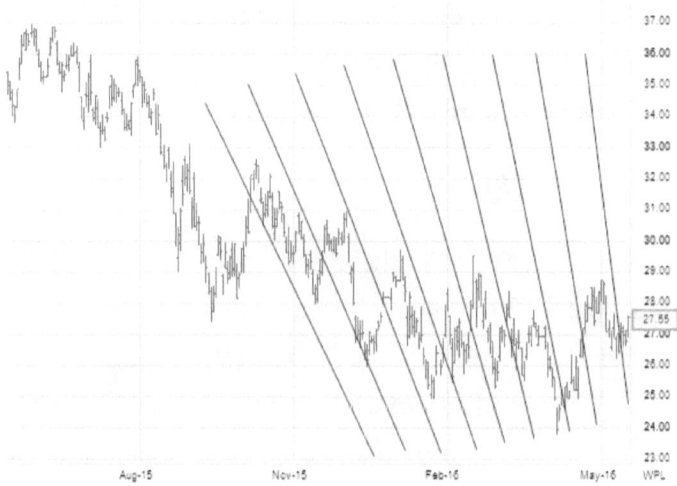

Image 58 is a daily chart which is intended to show how this chart and a weekly chart are related in terms of the placement of the TT3.

IMAGE 59 – WEEKLY CHART

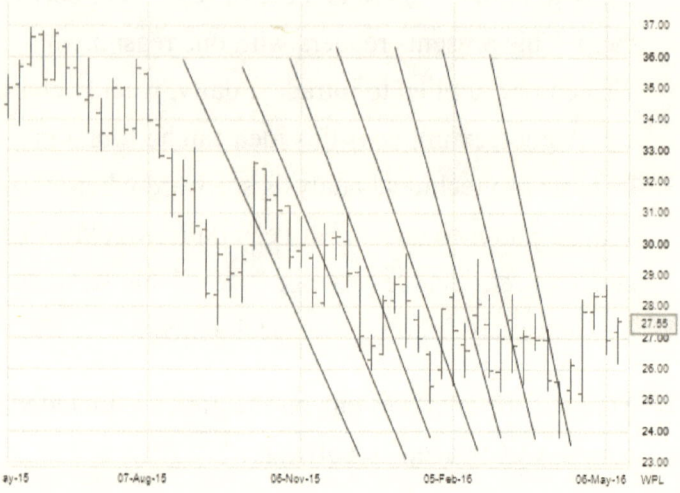

In image 59 it is clear that the TT3 lines are similarly located on this weekly chart of the same share. The only difference is that there are five times as many price bars in image 58 (five days in the week).

CONCLUSION

The images within these pages are examples of the use of the TT3 overlay. There are always several ways to place the overlay and it is the analyst's job to find an application that best suits their style of analysis. Day trading works provided the instrument is liquid and the bars on the chart are fully formed (high low close).

The overlay can be used in most if not all time frames and because we are measuring ratios that have already been imposed on the price bars, its scaling is not as critical as one might expect.

There is a degree of skill involved in placing the overlay so it would be wise to practice with the tool and perhaps test some of its suggested triggers to build confidence.

The TT3 overlay is intended to be an educational device primarily and it will provide the user with a greater understanding of the remarkable underlying geometry that drives world markets. The TT3 is not really predicting future activity even though it appears to be. It is simply identifying the location of a grid that imposes its influence on shares, commodities, currencies etc worldwide. Future price bars will bounce off the projected future grid lines when it is has been correctly located which can sometimes appear almost magical, especially when there is nothing but white space on the right hand side of the chart.

The main advantage of a physical overlay is that it can be quickly rotated and aligned with chart data allowing the user to quickly take a series of relevant measurements and not just one. This could be replicated in software and I will make the TT3 available to a few programmers. I would have to warn though that it might encourage laziness amongst analysts, many of whom would undoubtedly display a single TT3 fan ignoring the possible implications of other important fan measurements!

The TT3 can be obtained inexpensively from the web site or by email:

www.trendsandtripwires.com

tt3@trendsandtripwires.com

www.ingramcontent.com/pod-product-compliance
Lightning Source LLC
Chambersburg PA
CBHW022025170526
45157CB00003B/1350